KINGDOM
SPORTS

COLOSSIANS

THE COMPLETE COACH

A BIBLE STUDY FOR COACHES
WHO WANT TO UNDERSTAND
HOW GOD DEVELOPS AND SPIRITUALLY MATURES

A 12-WEEK STUDY

JOSHUA THIESSEN

Colossians - The Complete Coach

Cross Training Publishing

www.crosstrainingpublishing.com

(308) 293-3891

Copyright © 2024 by Joshua Thiessen

ISBN: 978-1-929478-80-4

FOREWORD

The Complete Coach: Book of Colossians study provides valuable lessons on and off the field. In the coaching world, where the pursuit of excellence meets the complexities of human potential, the Book of Colossians serves as a profound source of wisdom and inspiration. This Epistle, penned by the Apostle Paul, addresses fundamental themes of identity, purpose, and community—elements that resonate with coaches who strive to cultivate athletic skill, character, and resilience in their athletes.

The teachings found in Colossians encourage us to reflect on our own motivations and the impact we have on those we lead. Paul emphasizes the importance of grounding our efforts in faith and love, urging us to model these virtues in our coaching practices. As coaches, we are called to be mentors and role models, guiding our athletes not just in their sport but in their journey toward becoming well-rounded individuals. The principles of encouragement, accountability, toughness, and service highlighted in this letter can help us create an environment where athletes thrive both on and off the field.

Ron Brown
Nebraska Football Assistant Coach
Co-founder of Kingdom Sports

TABLE
OF
CONTENTS

THE COMPLETE COACH . . .

GRATITUDE

I am profoundly grateful to the Lord for the opportunity to study His Word, which continually points towards spiritual maturity in Christ. I'm also deeply thankful to everyone who played a role in editing, proofing, and laying out this study—their dedication is vital. My prayer is that this study will encourage the reader to grow in the wisdom and understanding which is only found in the Christ, and that God will use it to in your life so that you may be presented "fully mature in Christ" (Colossians 1:28).

INTRODUCTION

As a Christian coach, you are entrusted with more than just developing athletic skills—you are called to shape character and cultivate maturity in those we lead. The book of Colossians provides us with a profound blueprint for this task, as it reveals how the fullness of life is found in Christ. Paul's letter encourages us to help others grow into spiritual maturity, being "complete in Christ" (Colossians 2:10), where their identity, purpose, and strength are firmly rooted. This study will guide you through the essential truths of Colossians, equipping you to not only lead on the field but also foster deeper maturity and Christlikeness in your life and the lives of those you mentor, preparing them for challenges both in sports and in life.

Understanding Colossians

Understanding the context of Colossians is essential for grasping its message of spiritual maturity. Written by the Apostle Paul around AD 60-62 while he was imprisoned in Rome, Colossians addresses the believers in the small but growing church in Colossae, a city in Asia Minor (modern-day Turkey). Paul had not visited the church personally but wrote in response to reports from Epaphras, a fellow servant of Christ, who shared concerns about false teachings threatening the church. These teachings, often a mix of Jewish legalism, pagan mysticism, and early forms of Gnosticism, undermined the sufficiency of Christ. Paul's purpose in writing was to affirm Christ's preeminence and to remind the Colossians that true maturity and completeness can only be found in Him. This message remains essential for today as you seek to mature in Christ, resisting anything that would distract from His all-sufficient work.

Relevance to Coaches

1. **Christ-Centered Leadership:**

   - Coaches are called to lead with Christ at the center. Just as Christ is the head of the church, He should also be the foundation of how we lead, influence, and shape our teams. This means modeling Christlike character, humility, and service, ensuring that our leadership points others toward Him. But to model Christlikeness, the leader must realize how the Christian matures which comes from Christ Himself, where all the treasures of wisdom and knowledge are found.

2. **Growth over Scoreboard:**

   - Paul encourages believers to be "rooted and built up in Christ." This principle reminds us that the role of coach goes beyond developing physical or technical abilities or wins or loses. True success comes from how we conduct ourselves in God's economy.

3. **Pursuit of Excellence**

   - "Whatever you do, whether in word or deed, do it all in the name of the Lord Jesus." As coaches, pursuing excellence in both actions and words is not only essential, it is a theological imperative. The standard of true integrity is comprehensive in every area of life, both on and off the field.

4. **Build Strong, Christlike Relationships:**

   - Paul calls believers to "put on" virtues like compassion, kindness, humility, and patience and "put off" the old man's wrath, anger, malice, slander, and abusive speech. For coaches, fostering a team environment marked by these virtues is vital. By emphasizing what should be put off as well what attributes should be put on, the coach sets himself and his team for how to grow in Christ.

Key Themes to Explore

- **The Supremacy and Sufficiency of Christ:** Colossians emphasizes that Christ is supreme over all creation and fully sufficient for salvation and sanctification. Paul declares Christ as the image of the invisible God and the one in whom all things were created (Colossians 1:15-20). This theme underscores that believers need nothing beyond Christ for spiritual growth, rejecting false teachings that undermine His preeminence.

- **Spiritual Maturity in Christ:** A major theme in Colossians is growing into spiritual maturity. Paul encourages believers to be "rooted and built up in Him" (Colossians 2:7) and calls them to "put on" Christlike virtues (Colossians 3:12-14). This theme highlights the process of becoming complete in Christ, emphasizing spiritual growth and transformation in everyday life.

- **Putting off the Old, Putting on the New:** Another key theme in Colossians is the ongoing process of sanctification, where believers are called to "put off" the old self and "put on" the new self in Christ (Colossians 3:9-10). This transformation involves leaving behind sinful behaviors and attitudes— anger, malice, slander, and immorality—and replacing them with Christlike virtues such as compassion, kindness, humility, and love (Colossians 3:12-14). Sanctification is not a one-time event but an ongoing process as believers grow in spiritual maturity, aligning their character with Christ. Paul emphasizes that this change is empowered by the believer's new identity in Christ, and it affects every area of life, from personal relationships to public witness.

Conclusion

As you embark on this study of Colossians, approach each session with an open heart and mind, ready to uncover timeless truths that will deepen your spiritual maturity and strengthen your leadership both on and off the field. Colossians calls us to live lives that reflect the supremacy and sufficiency of Christ, challenging us to grow in wisdom, humility, and love. Through this study, may you come to better understand the sanctification process of putting off the old self and putting on the new self in Christ. I pray this study helps equip you and others toward spiritual maturity, grounded in a deeper relationship with Christ, and empowered to live for His glory in all you do.

Soli Deo Gloria,

Josh Thiessen

FORMAT

The format for this book is simple.
These are the parts of each chapter:

CHAPTER TITLE

Summarizes the key concept in one word or phrase.

STUDY STARTER

Helps you understand the importance and relevance of the spiritual truths you're about to study.

STUDY PASSAGE

Gives you the designated biblical text to read and study for the chapter.

STUDY HELP

Provides insight into the structure of the passage, meaning of words, interpretation of statements, and explanation of concepts.

STUDY QUESTIONS

Asks questions about the passage you must investigate and answer.

STUDY SUMMARY

Condenses the passage into one singular statement so you can understand the "big idea" of the text.

COACHING CONNECTION

Takes the Study Summary and transfers it to the world of coaching so you can clearly see the Spirit-intended applications of the Word of God in the life as a Christian coach.

KEYS TO WINNING

Guides you to meditate on the spiritual truths in the text and how they should shape your own heart and life as a coach.

GAME CHANGER

Points you to the person and work of Jesus Christ to help you be a complete coach through the power of the Gospel.

ONE BIG THING

Asks you to consider the most significant lesson you should take with you from the chapter.

IMPACT PRAYER

Motivates you to seek the Lord's help in applying the truths you have learned in each study.

STRATEGY

The strategy for this manual is also simple.
This is my recommendation:

Recruit a group of coaches to walk through the study with you. These coaches do not have to be Christians to join the study. As a matter of fact, I encourage you to reach out to any coach you think would consider participating.

Secure a copy of this training manual for every coach who participates in the study. You can order more copies at www.crosstrainingpublishing.com

Appoint a leader for the weekly group study. This leader can be a coach, former coach, spiritual leader, or pastor. The key criteria are that this person is a Christian who understands coaches, pursues Christ, and is willing to put in a little extra work to make the group study a powerful time in the Word of God. The group leader has the liberty to elaborate on the text and press into areas that are not necessarily covered in each lesson. This manual is merely a guide. There is freedom to take the study deeper and wider for more growth.

Schedule a weekly meeting day and time for 10-12 weeks. Allocate 45 to 60 minutes for the group study. Put the dates and times in your calendar and consider them a high priority.

Invest 30-60 minutes on your own prior to the study familiarizing yourself with the study passage, reading it, and answering the study questions. Consider the Study Summary, Coaching Connection, and Keys to Winning. Go to the group study ready to participate, ask questions, provide insight, seek help, and sharpen your fellow coaches in their pursuit of Christ.

Encourage one another throughout the week with the truths you are learning. As iron sharpens iron, so one coach will sharpen another.

Trust God to do a powerful work in your heart and life. The Word of God is living and active, sharper than a two-edged sword. It pierces to the division of soul and spirit, joints, and marrow, and discerns the thoughts and intentions of the heart. It will do heart surgery on you if you surrender yourself to it. So, give yourself to this study and watch God work powerfully in and through you in the details of your coaching and personal life.

Read the Scouting Report prior to Week One. Just as you try to know as much as you can about your opponent before you play them, you need to know as much as you can about the context of Colossians before you study it.

Don't worry if you can't find another coach to study with you. The best way to profit from this study is with a group of other coaches, but you can certainly do it on your own. If you're a Christian, you have the Spirit of Christ living in you. He will give you illumination along the way. So don't let your isolation from other like-minded coaches discourage you. We encourage you to ask your local pastor, FCA staff, or church leader to walk through it with you. Anyone who loves the Lord and wants to grow into greater maturity could be a great study partner.

★ ★ ★

SCOUTING REPORT

ON COLOSSIANS

The TITLE of Colossians

- The title "Colossians" refers to the recipients of the letter, the Christians in the city of Colossae. Situated in Asia Minor (modern-day Turkey), Colossae was a relatively small city with a growing church that had been established through the ministry of Epaphras, a co-laborer of the Apostle Paul. Though Paul had never personally visited the Colossian church, he wrote this letter to address their specific needs, including the threat of false teachings undermining the sufficiency of Christ. The title highlights the personal nature of Paul's communication, directed at a community of believers striving to live out their faith amidst cultural challenges. Through this letter, Paul exhorts the Colossians to grow in spiritual maturity, reminding them that Christ is preeminent over all creation and fully sufficient for their salvation and sanctification.

The AUTHORSHIP of Colossians

- The Apostle Paul is the author, as stated in the opening verse of the letter (Colossians 1:1). Written during Paul's imprisonment, likely in Rome around AD 60-62, this epistle is part of what is known as the "Prison Letters," along with Ephesians, Philippians, and Philemon. Paul's deep theological insight, pastoral care, and commitment to the gospel are evident throughout the letter, as he combats false teachings threatening the church and points the believers back to the sufficiency and supremacy of Christ. His passion for presenting believers as "mature in Christ" (Colossians 1:28) reflects the heart of his ministry and mission, which was to see the church strengthened and growing in faith.

The CENTRAL THEME of Colossians

- The theme of spiritual maturity is woven throughout the book of Colossians, as Paul continually emphasizes the believers' need to grow in their understanding and relationship with Christ. Paul frequently uses words like "full," "all," and "every" to express his desire for the Colossians to not just know Christ in part, but to know Him in full and be made complete in Him. In Colossians 1:9-10, Paul prays that they would be "filled with the knowledge of His will in all spiritual wisdom and understanding" and "bear fruit in every good work." Later, in Colossians 2:9-10, he declares that "in Christ all the fullness of the Deity lives in bodily form," and that believers "have been given fullness in Christ." This fullness and completeness are key aspects of spiritual maturity, which Paul aims for when he says his goal is to "present everyone fully mature in Christ" (Colossians 1:28). Paul understands that true maturity can only happen by looking to Christ, the source of all wisdom and knowledge, and living in light of His preeminence and sufficiency. The Colossians are called to reject false teachings and grow into full maturity by deepening their faith and understanding of Christ, who alone can make them complete.

The STRUCTURE of Colossians

- **Introduction and Thanksgiving (1:1-14)**

  a. Greeting and Salutation (1:1-2)

  ~ Paul introduces himself as the author and addresses the saints in Colossae.

  ~ Paul includes Timothy in his greeting.

  b. Thanksgiving and Prayer for Spiritual Growth (1:3-14)

  ~Paul expresses gratitude for the Colossians' faith, love, and hope.

  ~He prays for their continued growth in knowledge, wisdom, and strength.

  ~He highlights their deliverance and redemption in Christ.

- **The Supremacy and Sufficiency of Christ (1:15-2:7)**

  a. The Preeminence of Christ (1:15-20)

  ~ Christ's role in creation and His preeminence over all things.

  ~ Christ as the head of the church and the agent of reconciliation.

  b. Reconciliation through Christ (1:21-23)

  ~ The Colossians are reconciled to God through Christ's death.

  ~ Paul exhorts them to remain steadfast in the faith.

  c. Paul's Ministry for the Maturity of the Church (1:24-29)

  ~ Paul's sufferings are for the church's growth and maturity.

  ~ His labor is to present everyone fully mature in Christ.

  d. Encouragement to Walk in Christ (2:1-7)

  ~ Paul expresses his concern for the spiritual well-being of the Colossians.

  ~ He encourages them to walk in Christ, rooted and built up in Him, strengthened in faith.

- Warnings Against False Teachings (2:8-23)

  a. Rejecting Empty Philosophy (2:8-10)

    ~ Paul warns against deceptive philosophies and human traditions.

    ~ He emphasizes that all fullness dwells in Christ, and believers are complete in Him.

  b. The Fullness of Christ's Work (2:11-15)

    ~ Paul explains the spiritual circumcision believers experience in Christ.

    ~ Christ's victory over sin and spiritual powers through the cross.

  c. Freedom from Legalism (2:16-17)

    ~ Paul warns against legalistic judgments related to food, festivals, and Sabbath observance.

    ~ These are shadows; the reality is found in Christ.

  d. Avoiding False Asceticism (2:18-23)

    ~ Paul warns against ascetic practices and false humility.

    ~ Such regulations appear wise but lack value in restraining sinful behavior.

- The Christian Life: Putting on the New Self (3:1-4:6)

  a. Seek the Things Above (3:1-4)

    ~ Paul exhorts believers to set their hearts and minds on things above, not earthly things.

    ~ Their lives are hidden with Christ, awaiting His glorious return.

  b. Putting Off the Old Self (3:5-11)

    ~ Believers are called to put to death sinful behaviors such as sexual immorality, anger, and slander.

    ~ The old self is replaced by the new self, renewed in knowledge after the image of Christ.

  c. Putting On the New Self (3:12-17)

    ~ Paul exhorts the Colossians to clothe themselves with virtues like compassion, kindness, humility, and love.

    ~ The peace of Christ and the word of Christ should govern their lives as they live in gratitude.

  d. Christ-Centered Relationships (3:18-4:1)

    ~Instructions for households: Wives, husbands, children, and fathers are called to Christlike relationships.

~ Slaves and masters are given instructions on how to serve and lead in a Christ-honoring way.

    e. **Prayer and Wise Living (4:2-6)**

    ~ Paul calls for a devoted prayer life, praying for opportunities to proclaim the Gospel.

    ~ Believers are exhorted to live wisely before outsiders and to make the most of every opportunity.

- **Final Greetings and Instructions (4:7-18)**

    a. **Commendation of Paul's Coworkers (4:7-14)**

    ~ Paul sends greetings from his fellow workers, including Tychicus, Onesimus, Aristarchus, and others.

    ~ He highlights their faithful service and their concern for the Colossian church.

    b. **Instructions to the Church (4:15-17)**

    ~ Paul instructs the Colossians to share this letter with the Laodiceans and mentions his personal requests.

    ~ He encourages Archippus to fulfill his ministry.

    c. **Paul's Closing Words (4:18)**

    ~ Paul concludes with a personal signature, a reminder of his imprisonment, and a final blessing.

The STUDY of Colossians

How should we read and study Colossians today? When reading and studying Colossians today, we should approach it with a desire to deepen our understanding of Christ's supremacy and sufficiency, recognizing that Paul's call to spiritual maturity is just as relevant now as it was then. As we study, it's essential to reflect on how we can put off our old, sinful nature and actively put on the virtues of Christ, allowing His Word to shape our character, relationships, and daily actions. Colossians also challenges us to remain vigilant against modern "philosophies" and influences that undermine the Gospel, reminding us that we are complete in Christ alone. Ultimately, studying Colossians should lead to a deeper appreciation for the fullness of life found in Christ, encouraging us to grow in wisdom, faith, and devotion as we pursue spiritual maturity and live out our calling as followers of Jesus.

PREGAME QUESTIONS

1. **When you think of spiritual maturity, what comes to your mind?** What qualities, habits, or attitudes do you associate with being mature in your faith, both in your personal life and as a coach?

_____

_____

_____

_____

_____

_____

2. **Coaches often focus on developing athletes physically, but how often do we consider their spiritual growth?** How can coaching go beyond physical training to include developing character and spiritual maturity?

_____

_____

_____

_____

_____

_____

3. **What are some competing "philosophies" or influences that can distract you or those you coach from fully relying on Christ?** How do you think Colossians speaks to these distractions?

_____

_____

_____

_____

_____

_____

4. **At the end of this study in 12 weeks, what would you like to see God do in your heart and leadership?** What specific areas of growth do you hope to experience as a coach and follower of Christ?

_____

_____

_____

_____

_____

_____

5. **Colossians emphasizes being "rooted and built up in Christ" (Col. 2:7).** What does it mean for you to be "rooted" in Christ as a coach, and how does that influence how you lead others?

_____

_____

_____

_____

_____

_____

6. **Think of another coach or teammate who could be a partner in this study for mutual accountability, encouragement, and prayer.** Will you commit to walking through this study with them, holding each other accountable for growth in Christ and maturity as leaders? Write their name below and plan how you will support each other weekly.

_____

_____

_____

_____

_____

_____

NOTES:

THE COMPLETE COACH

REJOICES IN MATURITY

COLOSSIANS 1:1-8

STUDY STARTER

Coach Dabo Swinney, the head coach of Clemson University's football team, finds joy in the growth and maturity of his players. Known for his energetic personality and strong values, Swinney approaches coaching as an opportunity to make a meaningful impact on his players' lives, not just in their athletic performance but in their personal development. He frequently speaks about how rewarding it is to watch young athletes transform over their college careers, gaining confidence, discipline, and maturity on and off the field. For Swinney, every practice, game, and moment of hard work is a step toward something greater.

Swinney's commitment to his players' growth is evident in the culture he has built at Clemson. He focuses not only on wins and championships but also on the personal growth of each player. Swinney celebrates the small victories along the way, whether it's a player improving his academic performance, showing leadership among his peers, or demonstrating integrity in difficult situations. His joy in these moments creates a positive, encouraging environment that motivates players to strive for continuous improvement. Swinney's enthusiasm for their progress instills a sense of pride and purpose within his team, helping Clemson's athletes understand that their time in the program is about more than just football; it's about becoming the best version of themselves.

Coach Swinney's joy in his players' growth reflects the heart of Paul's message to the Colossians. In this passage, Paul expresses gratitude for the believers' faith, love, and maturity in the gospel, celebrating the growth he sees in their spiritual lives. Just as Swinney finds joy in the development of his players, Paul rejoices in the spiritual maturity of the Colossian church, recognizing that their progress is evidence of God's work within them and desiring for them to excel still more. This study should remind us that growth—whether in faith, character, or relationships—is worth celebrating, as it reflects God's ongoing work in our lives and others. Through Swinney's example and Paul's words, we are encouraged to find joy in the growth of others and in our own journey toward maturity.

STUDY PASSAGE

1 Paul, an apostle of Christ Jesus by the will of God, and Timothy our brother, 2 To the saints and faithful brothers in Christ at Colossae: Grace to you and peace from God our Father. 3 We always thank God, the Father of our Lord Jesus Christ, when we pray for you, 4 since we heard of your faith in Christ Jesus and of the love that you have for all the saints, 5 because of the hope laid up for you in heaven. Of this you have heard before in the word of the truth, the gospel, 6 which has come to you, as indeed in the whole world it is bearing fruit and increasing—as it also does among you, since the day you heard it and understood the grace of God in truth, 7 just as you learned it from Epaphras our beloved fellow servant. He is a faithful minister of Christ on your behalf 8 and has made known to us your love in the Spirit. (ESV)

STUDY HELP

- **"thankfulness"**—In Colossians 1:3, Paul expresses his thankfulness for the faith, love, and hope of the Colossian believers. Thankfulness is a theme in Paul's writings, reflecting his deep gratitude to God for the work He is doing in the lives of others. In this passage, Paul models how Christian leaders should cultivate an attitude of thankfulness, recognizing that the growth and fruitfulness in others' lives are ultimately the result of God's grace. This gratitude is not just a polite acknowledgment but a foundational posture of the heart, acknowledging God's ongoing work of transformation in believers.

- **"hope"**—Paul speaks of the "hope laid up for you in heaven" (Colossians 1:5), highlighting the future-oriented confidence that anchors the believers' faith and love. In the Bible, hope is more than a vague wish—it's a confident expectation rooted in God's promises. For the Colossians, this hope fuels their perseverance and shapes their daily lives as they look forward to the fulfillment of God's ultimate plan in Christ. This hope isn't limited to earthly successes or circumstances but is firmly secured in the eternal promises of God. For believers, hope offers motivation and endurance, knowing that the challenges of this life are temporary and that their ultimate reward is with Christ.

- *"word of truth"*—In Colossians 1:5, Paul refers to the "word of truth, the gospel" as the life-transforming message that has come to the Colossians and continues to bear fruit throughout the world. The "word of truth" is the gospel of Jesus Christ—God's revelation of salvation through His Son, which stands in stark contrast to the false teachings that were creeping into the Colossian church. This phrase emphasizes the reliability and power of the gospel to change lives and bring people to maturity in Christ.

STUDY QUESTIONS

1. In verses 3-4, Paul expresses thankfulness for the Colossians' faith and love. Why do you think Paul emphasizes these two qualities, and how are they connected to spiritual maturity in Christ?

_____

_____

_____

_____

2. Paul mentions that the Colossians' faith and love are rooted in the "hope laid up for you in heaven" (v. 5). How does the hope of eternal life influence the way you live now? In what ways does your understanding of heavenly hope affect your actions and priorities in your daily life and leadership?

_____

_____

_____

_____

3. In verse 5, Paul calls the gospel "the word of truth." What do you think Paul means by this phrase, and how does the truth of the gospel contrast with the false teachings threatening the Colossian church?

_____

_____

_____

_____

4. In verse 6, Paul says that the gospel is "bearing fruit and growing" throughout the world. What does it mean for the gospel to bear fruit, both globally and personally?

_____

_____

_____

_____

5. Paul acknowledges Epaphras' role in bringing the gospel to the Colossians (v. 7). What can we learn from Epaphras' faithfulness in sharing the gospel?

_____

_____

_____

_____

6. Verses 3-8 emphasize the interconnectedness of faith, love, and hope. How do these three qualities work together in the life of a believer? Which of these areas do you feel most called to grow in, and how can you cultivate that growth in your daily walk with Christ?

_____

_____

_____

_____

STUDY SUMMARY

Colossians 1:1-8 introduces Paul's letter with a focus on thankfulness for the Colossians' faith in Christ, love for others, and the hope they have in heaven. Paul highlights the transformative power of the gospel, which is bearing fruit globally and in their lives, urging them to remain rooted in these foundational truths as they continue to grow spiritually.

COACHING CONNECTION

The complete coach rejoices in the personal achievements and spiritual maturity of those they lead, celebrating the gospel's transformative work in their lives. This passage encourages coaches to focus on nurturing the whole person, finding fulfillment in the growth and development of others as they become more rooted in Christ.

KEYS TO WINNING

▶ **VIDEO GUIDE AT KINGDOMSPORTS.ONLINE**

▶ THANKFULNESS FOR SPIRITUAL GROWTH

Paul expresses deep gratitude for the faith, love, and hope evident in the Colossians' lives, reminding us to be thankful for the spiritual growth and maturity we see in others.

1. How often do you take the time to thank God for the spiritual growth you see in those around you, whether teammates, colleagues, or those you lead? Reflect on a specific instance where you've seen someone grow in faith, love, or hope—how did you respond, and how can you cultivate a heart of thankfulness for such moments?

_____

_____

_____

2. Reflect on a specific instance where you've seen someone grow in faith, love, or hope—how did you respond, and how can you cultivate a heart of thankfulness for such moments?

_____

_____

_____

_____

▶ THE TRANSFORMING POWER OF THE GOSPEL

The gospel is described as "bearing fruit and growing" both in Colossae and around the world, highlighting its ongoing transformative power in the lives of believers.

1. How have you personally experienced the transforming power of the gospel in your life, and how is it continuing to bear fruit in your daily actions and relationships?

_____

_____

_____

_____

2. In what ways are you actively allowing the gospel to "grow and bear fruit" through your influence on others, whether in your family, team, or community? Consider how you can further share the gospel's transformative power, helping others experience spiritual growth and maturity.

_____

_____

_____

_____

▶ THE IMPORTANCE OF FAITH, LOVE, AND HOPE

These three foundational virtues—faith in Christ, love for others, and hope in the promises of God—are central to the Christian life and a key focus for personal and communal spiritual maturity.

1. Which of these three virtues—faith, love, or hope—do you feel is strongest in your life right now, and which one do you feel needs further growth?

_____

_____

_____

_____

2. How are you actively cultivating faith, love, and hope in those you lead or mentor, whether in your personal life, team, or church?

_____

_____

_____

_____

GAME CHANGER

Paul begins his letter with a spirit of gratitude for the faith, love, and hope evident in the Colossian believers' lives. This passage reminds us of the importance of recognizing the spiritual growth in others and ourselves. Just as Paul rejoiced in seeing these virtues flourish in the Colossians, we should also cultivate a heart of thankfulness for the work God is doing in and through His people. By focusing on these qualities—faith in Christ, love for others, and hope in the promises of God—we are encouraged to reflect on how these virtues shape our daily lives and relationships.

The gospel is central to this transformation. Paul notes that the "word of truth, the gospel," is bearing fruit and growing, both in Colossae and around the world. This ongoing growth reminds us that the gospel is not a static message but an active and powerful force that continues to change lives. When we open ourselves to the gospel's work, we experience its transformative power—leading us to deeper faith, genuine love for others, and an unshakable hope in the future God has promised. The gospel doesn't just bring salvation; it fosters ongoing spiritual maturity, molding us more into the image of Christ.

Ultimately, Colossians 1:1-8 points us back to the heart of the gospel, reminding us that all spiritual growth comes through Christ. We are called to rely fully on Him, knowing He is the source of our faith, love, and hope. As we grow in these areas, we bear witness to the power of the gospel, allowing its fruit to be visible in our lives. This passage challenges us to stay rooted in Christ, to be thankful for His work, and to live in a way that reflects the transformative message of the gospel to those around us.

ONE BIG THING

What is the most significant lesson for you to take with you from this chapter?

_____

_____

_____

_____

_____

_____

_____

_____

_____

IMPACT PRAYER

Heavenly Father, thank You for the powerful reminder in Colossians of the faith, love, and hope You cultivate in us through the gospel. Help us to recognize and rejoice in the spiritual growth happening in our lives and in the lives of others. May we always be thankful for the work You are doing, shaping us into the image of Christ. As the gospel continues to bear fruit in the world, let it transform our hearts and deepen our faith, love, and hope. Keep us rooted in You. Amen

NOTES:

★ ★ ★

CHAPTER TWO
THE COMPLETE COACH
PRAYS FOR MATURITY

COLOSSIANS 1:9-14

STUDY STARTER

Coach Mark Richt, known for his strong faith and commitment to his players' personal growth, has always placed a high value on praying for the maturity of those he leads. Throughout his coaching career at the University of Georgia and the University of Miami, Richt was open about his desire to see his players develop as athletes and individuals with purpose and integrity. For Richt, success was more than wins and championships; it was about guiding young men to become strong, resilient, and grounded in their values. He regularly prayed for his players, asking God to grant them wisdom, strength, and a heart for others, believing that these qualities would carry them through life far beyond the football field.

Richt's prayers for his players were a testament to his commitment to their spiritual growth. He understood that college was a pivotal time for young men, and he wanted his players to leave the program prepared for sports and life. He encouraged them to reflect on who they were becoming and make choices aligned with their faith and values. Through Bible studies, team devotionals, and personal mentorship, Richt taught his players to seek God's guidance in all areas of life. His dedication to their personal development inspired many of his athletes to pursue deeper faith, recognizing—as Richt shared on the North Carolina Baptists podcast—that true success is rooted in character, not just performance.

As we study Colossians 1:9-14, Coach Richt's commitment to praying for his players' growth provides a powerful illustration of Paul's prayer for the Colossian church. In this passage, Paul asks that the believers be "filled with the knowledge of His will," strengthened with patience and endurance, and overflowing with gratitude. Similarly, Richt's prayers for his players extended far beyond their success on the field; he prayed for their long-term growth and maturity, hoping they would reflect God's love and wisdom in their lives. This study invites us to consider the importance of praying not only for our own needs or physical needs but, most importantly, for the spiritual growth of those around us, seeking God's guidance and strength in our collective journey of faith.

STUDY PASSAGE

1 *⁹ And so, from the day we heard, we have not ceased to pray for you, asking that you may be filled with the knowledge of his will in all spiritual wisdom and understanding, ¹⁰ so as to walk in a manner worthy of the Lord, fully pleasing to him: bearing fruit in every good work and increasing in the knowledge of God; ¹¹ being strengthened with all power, according to his glorious might, for all endurance and patience with joy; ¹²] giving thanks to the Father, who has qualified you to share in the inheritance of the saints in light. ¹³ He has delivered us from the domain of darkness and transferred us to the kingdom of his beloved Son, ¹⁴ in whom we have redemption, the forgiveness of sins. (ESV)*

STUDY HELP

- *"knowledge"*—In verse 9, Paul prays that the Colossians may be filled with the "knowledge of His will." In the book of Colossians, the Apostle Paul emphasizes the concept of "knowledge," particularly the knowledge of God's will and the knowledge of Christ Himself. This emphasis serves as a foundation for spiritual maturity and safeguards against false teachings infiltrating the church in Colossae.

- *"wisdom"*—Paul emphasizes "wisdom" as a crucial component of spiritual maturity and a safeguard against false teachings. Wisdom, in Paul's context, is not merely human intellect or philosophical reasoning but divine insight granted by God through the Holy Spirit.

- *"redemption"*—The term "redemption" refers to the act of being set free from bondage through the payment of a ransom. In Colossians, Paul weaves this theme to highlight the sufficiency of Christ's sacrifice and its implications for spiritual maturity and daily living.

STUDY QUESTIONS

1. In verse 9, Paul prays that the Colossians may be "filled with the knowledge of His will in all spiritual wisdom and understanding." What does it mean to be "filled with the knowledge of His will" and how do "spiritual wisdom and understanding" differ from worldly wisdom, and why are they important for spiritual maturity?

_____

_____

_____

_____

2. How can we live a life worthy of the Lord and please Him in every way, bearing fruit in every good work and growing in the knowledge of God, as emphasized in verse 10?

_____

_____

_____

_____

3. Why is it essential for believers to be strengthened with all power according to His glorious might, as mentioned in verse 11, and how does this enable us to exhibit endurance and patience in challenging situations?

_____

_____

_____

_____

4. What does it mean that God has "qualified" us to share in the inheritance of His holy people, as stated in verses 12-14, and how does understanding our inheritance inspire gratitude and influence the way we live)?

_____

_____

_____

_____

5. How does being rescued from the dominion of darkness and brought into the kingdom of the Son He loves, as described in verse 13, change our perspective on life, and in what ways does recognizing our transfer into Christ's kingdom affect our priorities and goals?

_____

_____

_____

_____

6. Considering that this passage highlights themes of spiritual growth, transformation, and gratitude, how does Paul's prayer model how we should pray for ourselves and others regarding spiritual maturity, and how does embracing these principles influence your approach to leadership, mentorship, and personal development?

_____

_____

_____

_____

STUDY SUMMARY

In Colossians 1:9-14, Paul prays for the Colossians to be filled with the knowledge of God's will through spiritual wisdom and understanding, so they may live lives worthy of the Lord, bearing fruit in every good work and growing in the knowledge of God. He emphasizes the importance of being strengthened with God's power to endure with patience and joyfully give thanks to the Father, who has qualified them to share in the inheritance of the saints by delivering them from darkness and redeeming them through His Son.

COACHING CONNECTION

The complete coach deeply understands God's will through spiritual wisdom in Scripture, lives a life worthy of the Lord by bearing fruit in good works, and continually grows in the knowledge of God. Relying on God's strength, the coach exhibits endurance and patience, maintains a joyful and thankful heart, and leads with integrity, inspiring spiritual growth in others while navigating challenges with divine guidance and gratitude.

KEYS TO WINNING

▶ VIDEO GUIDE AT KINGDOMSPORTS.ONLINE

▶ THE IMPORTANCE OF KNOWING GOD'S WILL

Paul prays for the Colossians to be filled with the knowledge of God's will through all spiritual wisdom and understanding (verse 9). This emphasizes that spiritual maturity begins with a deep understanding of God's desires and purposes. Knowing God's will enables believers to align their lives with His plans and designs.

1. How are you intentionally seeking to be filled with the knowledge of God's will through spiritual wisdom and understanding in your daily life?

_____

_____

_____

_____

2. In what areas of your life do you feel closely aligned with God's plans, and where might there be misalignment or uncertainty about His will?

_____

_____

_____

_____

▶ LIVING A LIFE WORTHY OF THE LORD

The passage highlights that understanding God's will should result in action—living a life worthy of the Lord and pleasing Him in every way (verse 10). This includes bearing fruit in every good work and growing in the knowledge of God. It underscores the connection between knowledge and practice, showing that true understanding manifests in ethical behavior and continual spiritual growth.

1. In what areas of your life do you feel you are effectively living a life worthy of the Lord, bearing fruit in good works, and where might you need to improve to align more closely with His will?

_____

_____

_____

_____

2. How does your understanding of God's will translate into practical actions in your daily life, and what steps can you take to ensure that your knowledge leads to ethical behavior and spiritual growth?

_____

_____

_____

_____

3. What disciplines or routines can you establish to continue growing in the knowledge of God, and how might this ongoing growth influence the way you live and interact with others?

_____

_____

_____

_____

▶ STRENGTH AND ENDURANCE THROUGH GOD'S POWER

Paul emphasizes the need to be strengthened with all power according to God's glorious might so believers may have great endurance and patience (verse 11). This takeaway reminds us that spiritual strength and the ability to persevere through challenges come from relying on God's power rather than our own. It encourages maintaining a joyful and thankful heart, recognizing that God has rescued and brought us into His kingdom (verses 12-14).

1. In which areas of your life are you relying on your own strength instead of seeking God's power for endurance and patience?

_____

_____

_____

_____

2. How does recognizing that God has rescued and brought you into His kingdom influence you to maintain a joyful and thankful heart during difficult times?

_____

_____

_____

_____

GAME CHANGER

The Apostle Paul offers a heartfelt prayer for believers to be filled with the knowledge of God's will through all spiritual wisdom and understanding. This passage invites the reader to go beyond mere intellectual acknowledgment. By earnestly knowing and pursuing God's revealed will in Scripture, we align ourselves with His divine purpose, allowing His wisdom to guide our decisions and actions. This alignment transforms our daily walk, enabling us to live lives worthy of the Lord, bearing fruit in every good work and growing continuously in our knowledge of Him.

As we are strengthened with all power according to His glorious might, we develop great endurance and patience. Divine strength is not something we muster on our own; it is a gracious gift from God that empowers us to overcome obstacles with a joyful and thankful heart. Recognizing that we have been qualified to share in this inheritance it should fill us with gratitude and reinforce our identity as beloved children of God. This gratitude propels us to live out our faith authentically, reflecting God's love and grace to those around us.

This passage is a reminder of the power of the gospel—the good news of Jesus Christ. God has rescued us from the dominion of darkness and brought us into the kingdom of His beloved Son, in whom we have redemption and the forgiveness of sins. This rescue is at the heart of the gospel message: through Jesus' sacrifice, we are redeemed and restored to a right relationship with God. Understanding this truth transforms our perspective as we realize that our ability to know God's will, live worthy lives, and be strengthened by His power is made possible through Christ's redemptive work.

ONE BIG THING

What is the most significant lesson for you to take with you from this chapter?

_____

_____

_____

_____

_____

_____

_____

_____

IMPACT PRAYER

Heavenly Father, thank You for filling us with the knowledge of Your will through all spiritual wisdom and understanding. Help us align with Your divine purpose, guiding our decisions so we may live lives worthy of You, bearing fruit in every good work. Strengthen us with Your glorious might, granting us endurance and patience, and fill our hearts with gratitude for rescuing us through the redemption and forgiveness found in Jesus Christ. In Jesus' name, Amen.

NOTES:

★ ★ ★

CHAPTER THREE
THE COMPLETE COACH
EXALTS CHRIST

COLOSSIANS 1:15-20

STUDY STARTER

Tim Tebow, known for his unwavering faith as much as his athletic achievements, exemplifies what it means to exalt Christ both on and off the field. From his college football days at the University of Florida, where he led the team to two national championships, to his time in the NFL and beyond, Tebow has consistently pointed others to Christ. He gained national attention for his "Tebowing" stance—kneeling in prayer during games—which he used as a moment to thank God and bring focus to his faith. His willingness to openly pray and acknowledge God during the height of his athletic career showed a deep commitment to keeping Christ at the center, despite public scrutiny or pressure to conform.

Off the field, Tebow continues to exalt Christ through his charity work, public speaking, and writing. His foundation, the Tim Tebow Foundation, is dedicated to serving vulnerable populations, including children with special needs, orphans, and those struggling with illness. One of the foundation's signature events, "Night to Shine," is a prom night for people with special needs held worldwide, and Tebow sees it as a way to honor Christ's love for all people. In his books *Shaken* and *This Is the Day*, Tebow shares how he navigates challenges by placing his trust in God and viewing his life as a platform to spread Christ's message. He speaks openly about how his purpose is not defined by sports but by his relationship with Christ, demonstrating how he seeks to exalt God in all he does.

His life mirrors the message of Colossians 1:15-20, where Christ is exalted as the Creator, Sustainer, and the One in whom "all things hold together." Just as this passage calls believers to see Christ as supreme in every aspect, Tebow's journey illustrates a life centered on exalting Christ. His actions, both in his athletic career and philanthropic efforts, reflect a deep desire to honor Jesus in every opportunity. For Tebow, faith is not just part of his identity—it is his foundation, shaping everything he does and serving as a powerful example of what it means to worship Christ fully in every sphere of life.

STUDY PASSAGE

1 *15 He is the image of the invisible God, the firstborn of all creation. 16 For by him all things were created, in heaven and on earth, visible and invisible, whether thrones or dominions or rulers or authorities—all things were created through him and for him. 17 And he is before all things, and in him all things hold together. 18 And he is the head of the body, the church. He is the beginning, the firstborn from the dead, that in everything he might be preeminent. 19 For in him all the fullness of God was pleased to dwell, 20 and through him to reconcile to himself all things, whether on earth or in heaven, making peace by the blood of his cross. (ESV).*

STUDY HELP

- *"image"*— This word emphasizes that Jesus perfectly represents and reveals the nature of God to humanity. Studying "image" helps you understand the concept of Christ being the visible manifestation of the invisible God, which is central to grasping His divinity and role in salvation.

- *"firstborn"*—The term "firstborn" signifies supremacy and preeminence rather than chronological birth order. Exploring this word allows you to delve into Christ's authority over all creation and His unique status as supreme above all things, highlighting His eternal existence and sovereignty.

- *"fullness"*—"Fullness" indicates that the complete nature and essence of God reside in Christ. Highlighting this word helps you comprehend the completeness of Christ's deity and how He embodies all the attributes of God, reinforcing the doctrine of the Trinity.

STUDY QUESTIONS

1. What does it mean that Christ is "the image of the invisible God" (verse 15)? How does this concept help us understand the nature of God and His revelation to humanity through Jesus?

_____

_____

_____

_____

2. How should you interpret the term "firstborn over all creation" (verse 15)? What are the implications of this title for understanding Christ's authority over all things?

_____

_____

_____

_____

3. What is the significance of all things being created "through Him and for Him" (verse 16)? How does recognizing Christ as the agent and purpose of creation affect our view of the world and our place in it?

_____

_____

_____

_____

4. How does Christ "hold all things together," and what does this reveal about His ongoing relationship with creation?

_____

_____

_____

_____

5. What does it mean that Christ is "the head of the body, the church" and "the beginning and the firstborn from among the dead" (verse 18)?

_____

_____

_____

_____

6. Why was God pleased to have "all His fullness dwell in Him" and to "reconcile to Himself all things" through Christ and what are the implications for believers?

_____

_____

_____

_____

STUDY SUMMARY

Colossians 1:15-20 proclaims the supremacy and deity of Jesus Christ, stating that He is the image of the invisible God and the firstborn over all creation. This passage emphasizes that all things were created through Him and for Him, and through His fullness, God reconciled all things to Himself, highlighting Christ's central role in creation and redemption.

COACHING CONNECTION

The complete coach proclaims the supremacy and full deity of Jesus Christ, emphasizing that He is the image of the invisible God and the creator and sustainer of all things. This means placing Christ at the center of your coaching philosophy, modeling His character in your interactions, and relying on His guidance to lead.

KEYS TO WINNING

▶ VIDEO GUIDE AT KINGDOMSPORTS.ONLINE

▶ THE SUPREMACY AND PREEMINENCE OF CHRIST IN CREATION

Recognizing the supremacy and preeminence of Christ means placing Jesus at the center of your coaching philosophy and practice. Understanding that all things were created through Him and for Him (Colossians 1:16) instructs you to align your goals and methods with His purposes. This perspective transforms coaching into a form of worship, where every training session, game, and interaction becomes an opportunity to honor Christ.

1. How can you intentionally place Jesus at the center of your coaching philosophy and daily practice, recognizing His supremacy and preeminence in all things?

_____

_____

_____

_____

2. In what ways does understanding that all things were created through Him and for Him influence your approach to setting goals and interacting with your team?

_____

_____

_____

_____

▶ CHRIST AS THE SUSTAINER AND HEAD OF THE CHURCH

Knowing that Christ is before all things and that in Him all things hold together provides a foundation of trust and reliance on His sustaining power. You can find confidence and peace in the fact that Jesus is the ultimate leader—the head of the body, the church

(Colossians 1:18). This understanding encourages you to depend on His wisdom and strength rather than solely on your abilities

1. How does recognizing that Christ is before all things and that in Him all things hold together influence your trust and reliance on His sustaining power? Reflect on specific areas where you may have been relying primarily on your own abilities.

_____

_____

_____

_____

2. In what ways can acknowledging Jesus as the ultimate leader—the head of the body, the church—bring confidence and peace to your role as a coach, and how might this understanding impact your interactions with your team?

_____

_____

_____

_____

▸ THE FULLNESS OF GOD DWELLING IN CHRIST AND RECONCILIATION TO GOD THROUGH HIM

Embracing the truth that all the fullness of God dwells in Christ and that through Him, God reconciles all things empowers you to be an ambassador of reconciliation in your coaching role. Recognizing the completeness and sufficiency of Christ's sacrifice motivates you to foster an environment of grace, forgiveness, and restoration within your team. When conflicts arise, you can lead by example in pursuing peace and facilitating healing conversations.

1. How does the understanding that all the fullness of God dwells in Christ and that He reconciles all things to Himself inspire you to promote grace, forgiveness, and restoration in relationships?

_____

_____

_____

_____

2. In what practical ways can you be an ambassador of reconciliation in your life, especially during times of tension or disagreement?

_____

_____

_____

_____

GAME CHANGER

Colossians 1:15-20 reveals Christ's supremacy and centrality in creation and redemption, proclaiming that Jesus is "the image of the invisible God" and the one in whom "all things hold together." This truth calls us to recognize Jesus not only as a historical figure but as the sovereign Lord who intimately sustains all of creation. For each of us, this understanding transforms our daily lives, reminding us that everything—our work, relationships, challenges, and achievements—finds its purpose and cohesion in Him. Knowing that Christ holds all things together reassures us in uncertain times, anchoring our trust in His sustaining power rather than in fleeting circumstances.

As the "firstborn over all creation," Christ is not only supreme over the world but also the head of the church, leading us in spiritual growth and unity. His role as head shapes how we approach our relationships, calling us to reflect His character in every interaction and to pursue lives that honor Him. This passage challenges us to see our lives as a reflection of His love and grace, demonstrating humility, patience, and forgiveness as we strive to live out our faith. By aligning our lives with His example, we become conduits of His peace, fostering reconciliation and unity in our families, communities, and workplaces.

God has reconciled all things to Himself, making peace through Christ's shed blood on the cross. This reconciliation changes everything—it means that no sin or failure can separate us from God's love. Embracing this gospel truth invites us to live with gratitude, knowing that Christ's all-sufficient sacrifice has secured our peace with God. As we grasp the fullness of God dwelling in Christ and His reconciling power, we are inspired to live boldly, letting His love and grace shape every aspect of our lives.

ONE BIG THING

What is the most significant lesson for you to take with you from this chapter?

IMPACT PRAYER

Lord Jesus, we praise You as the image of the invisible God, the one who holds all things together and leads us in peace and unity. Help us to recognize Your supreme place in every part of our lives and to live with hearts anchored in Your sustaining power, especially in uncertain times. Thank You for reconciling us to the Father through Your sacrifice, bringing us peace and purpose. May we reflect Your love, grace, and humility in our interactions, living boldly and gratefully for You. In Your name, we pray, Amen.

★ ★ ★

CHAPTER FOUR

THE COMPLETE COACH

REMAINS STEADFAST

COLOSSIANS 1:21-23

STUDY STARTER

Coach Tom Osborne exemplified steadfastness and faithfulness throughout his 25-season tenure as head coach at the University of Nebraska. Leading the team to three national championships and consistently high rankings, Osborne's success was rooted in his coaching skill and unyielding commitment to his values. Win or lose, Osborne held firmly to his principles, never compromising his integrity or allowing the pressures of competition to sway his dedication to his faith and character. He approached every game and season with a calm resolve, focusing on his players' well-being and the program's integrity.

Osborne's faithfulness extended far beyond the field and was evident in the personal care he showed each player. He saw his role as an opportunity to mentor young men, instilling values that would guide them beyond their football careers. Rather than focusing solely on performance, Osborne emphasized character, discipline, and respect, encouraging his players to embody these qualities in all aspects of life. Many of his former athletes credit him with shaping their lives, noting the lasting impact of his faithful adherence to these values and his dedication to their personal growth.

As we study Colossians 1:21-23, Coach Osborne's life exemplifies living with steadfastness and faithfulness. Just as Paul urges believers to hold firmly to the hope of the gospel, Osborne's life demonstrates a commitment to standing strong in faith and conviction, even in the face of pressure. His legacy goes beyond his football achievements, defined by his faithfulness to God's call to mentor and lead with integrity. Osborne's story encourages us to remain grounded in our faith, reminding us that steadfastness and faithfulness reach beyond immediate outcomes to influence lives and leave a legacy of hope and trust in God's promises.

STUDY PASSAGE

1 *21 And you, who once were alienated and hostile in mind, doing evil deeds, 22 he has now reconciled in his body of flesh by his death, in order to present you holy and blameless and above reproach before him, 23 if indeed you continue in the faith, stable and steadfast, not shifting from the hope of the gospel that you heard, which has been proclaimed in all creation under heaven, and of which I, Paul, became a minister. (ESV)*

STUDY HELP

- *"alienated"*—This word emphasizes the separation between humanity and God due to sin. Studying "alienated" helps you see the significant impact of sin on your relationship with God and the need for reconciliation.

- *"reconciled"*—"Reconciled" points to the restoration of the relationship between God and humanity through Christ's sacrifice. This word is central to understanding the gospel and the work Christ accomplished on the cross.

- *"holy"*—"Holy" describes the transformed state believers are called to through Christ. It emphasizes that, in reconciliation, God doesn't merely forgive but sanctifies, setting believers apart as righteous and without blemish.

STUDY QUESTIONS

1. What does it mean to be "alienated" from God, and how does this concept help us understand the impact of sin on our relationship with Him?

_____

_____

_____

_____

2. How does Paul's description of us as "enemies in your minds because of your evil behavior" emphasize the need for internal as well as external transformation?

_____

_____

_____

_____

3. What does it mean that we have been "reconciled" to God by Christ's physical body through death, and why is this sacrifice essential for restoring our relationship with God?

_____

_____

_____

_____

4. How does being presented "holy, without blemish and free from accusation" impact your view of yourself and your relationship with God?

_____

_____

_____

_____

5. In verse 23, Paul stresses the importance of continuing in the faith, established and firm. Why is ongoing commitment to the faith essential, even after reconciliation with God?

_____

_____

_____

_____

6. What practical steps can you take to "not move from the hope held out in the gospel" as Paul encourages in verse 23?

_____

_____

_____

_____

STUDY SUMMARY

Colossians 1:21-23 highlights the transformation believers experience through Christ: though once alienated from God and hostile in mind, they are now reconciled through Jesus' death to be presented holy and blameless before Him. This passage emphasizes the importance of continuing in faith, grounded in the hope of the gospel.

COACHING CONNECTION

The complete coach emphasizes the importance of recognizing the transformative power of Christ's reconciliation, moving from alienation to a holy and blameless life, and strives to remain steadfast in that truth no matter what else is going on.

KEYS TO WINNING

▶ **VIDEO GUIDE AT KINGDOMSPORTS.ONLINE**

▶ TRANSFORMATION THROUGH RECONCILIATION

This passage reminds us that, though we were once alienated from God and hostile in mind, Christ's sacrifice has reconciled us to God. This transformative reconciliation changes our identity and restores our relationship with God, allowing us to live in peace with Him.

1. How does understanding that Christ's sacrifice has moved you from a place of alienation to reconciliation with God impact how you see yourself and your relationship with Him?

_____

_____

_____

_____

2. In what ways can you allow the peace that comes from reconciliation with God to shape your actions, relationships, and responses to challenges?

_____

_____

_____

_____

▶ THE NEW IDENTITY IN CHRIST

Through Christ's death, believers are presented as "holy, without blemish, and free from accusation" before God. This new identity encourages us to view ourselves through the lens of God's grace, recognizing that we are seen as pure and beloved in His eyes.

1. How does knowing that you are viewed by God as "holy, without blemish, and free from accusation" change the way you see yourself and approach your daily life? In what areas of your life could this truth bring greater freedom or peace?

_____

_____

_____

_____

2. In what ways can viewing yourself through the lens of God's grace help you extend that same grace to others?

_____

_____

_____

_____

▶ THE CALL TO PERSEVERE IN FAITH

Paul urges believers to continue in the faith, grounded and steadfast, highlighting the importance of perseverance. This takeaway emphasizes that while reconciliation is a gift, maintaining a close relationship with God requires an ongoing commitment to the hope of the gospel.

1. What does it mean to be "grounded and steadfast" in your faith, and how can you actively cultivate this perseverance in your daily life?

_____

_____

_____

_____

2. How does viewing reconciliation as a gift and a call to perseverance shape your approach to your relationship with God?

_____

_____

_____

_____

GAME CHANGER

Colossians 1:21-23 reminds us that, before knowing Christ, we were "alienated" from God, separated by sin and hostile in mind. This alienation wasn't just about actions; it was a complete separation from God. Realizing the impact of sin on our relationship with God can be sobering. However, this passage highlights that through Jesus' sacrifice, God reconciled us to Himself, bridging that separation.

In Christ, we are not only forgiven but also given a new identity: "holy, without blemish, and free from accusation" before God. This reconciliation doesn't merely cover our past mistakes; it transforms how God views us—pure, beloved, and accepted. For many, embracing this new identity takes faith and intentional reflection, especially when we may still feel imperfect. But this truth calls us to view ourselves through the lens of God's grace, letting go of accusations or guilt that may weigh on us. Through Christ, we stand unblemished before God, enabling us to approach Him with confidence, assured of our place in His family.

While Christ's sacrifice is sufficient for our redemption and security, we are called to perseverance daily. This daily faith walk involves cultivating habits like prayer, Scripture reading, and fellowship. As we stay rooted in the truth of our reconciliation, we reflect God's love to others, ministering to them with the transformative power of the gospel that made peace with God possible.

ONE BIG THING

What is the most significant lesson for you to take with you from this chapter?

_____

_____

_____

_____

_____

_____

_____

_____

_____

_____

_____

_____

_____

_____

_____

IMPACT PRAYER

Lord, thank You for reconciling me to Yourself through Christ, transforming my identity from alienated to beloved, holy, and blameless. Help me to see myself through the lens of Your grace, letting go of guilt and resting in the assurance of Your love. Strengthen me to stay grounded and steadfast in faith, continually rooted in the hope of the gospel. May my life reflect Your love and grace. In Jesus' name, Amen.

NOTES:

★ ★ ★

CHAPTER FIVE
THE COMPLETE COACH

LABORS FOR OTHERS TO MATURE

COLOSSIANS 1:24-29

STUDY STARTER

In 2019, after leading the University of Virginia men's basketball team to its first-ever NCAA Championship, Coach Tony Bennett made a remarkable decision that captured the spirit of selfless dedication. When offered a substantial pay raise as a reward for his success, Bennett declined it, asking instead that the funds be directed to benefit his players and program. His request was simple: he wanted resources to be used to improve facilities, provide additional opportunities for his athletes, and support his staff. This gesture was an example of Bennett's commitment to laboring not for personal gain but for the growth and well-being of those he leads.

Bennett's choice to sacrifice a personal financial reward demonstrated his deep commitment to his players' development, both on and off the court. He understood that meaningful growth comes from investing in a strong foundation, and he was willing to forego personal comfort to make that happen for his team. By redirecting the funds to resources that would serve his players, Bennett was showing that his role as a coach went far beyond winning championships. His focus was on creating an environment that fostered growth, teamwork, and character—qualities that would help his players long after their time in college.

In Colossians 1:24-29, Paul speaks of joyfully laboring and even suffering so that others might grow in maturity. Bennett's decision to sacrifice his own reward for the benefit of his team reflects this same spirit of toil and dedication. By choosing to prioritize his players' needs over his own, Bennett exemplifies a commitment to servant leadership, working tirelessly to uplift and support those in his care. His actions remind us that true leadership often requires sacrifice and a willingness to set aside personal gains to invest in the well-being and growth of others. As we study this passage, Bennett's example encourages us to labor with purpose, aiming to build others up in ways that honor God and lead to lasting impact.

STUDY PASSAGE

1 [24] Now I rejoice in my sufferings for your sake, and in my flesh I am filling up what is lacking in Christ's afflictions for the sake of his body, that is, the church, [25] of which I became a minister according to the stewardship from God that was given to me for you, to make the word of God fully known, [26] the mystery hidden for ages and generations but now revealed to his saints. [27] To them God chose to make known how great among the Gentiles are the riches of the glory of this mystery, which is Christ in you, the hope of glory. [28] Him we proclaim, warning everyone and teaching everyone with all wisdom, that we may present everyone mature in Christ. [29] For this I toil, struggling with all his energy that he powerfully works within me. (ESV)

STUDY HELP

- *"sufferings*—Paul's willingness to endure suffering for the sake of the church highlights the cost of discipleship and ministry.

- *"mystery*—"Mystery" refers to the previously hidden truth of the gospel that has now been revealed through Christ. This term demonstrates the nature of the unfolding plan of God and the significance of Christ's work being made known.

- *"maturity"*—Paul's goal in ministry is to present believers as mature in Christ, highlighting spiritual growth as a central focus of the Christian journey. Maturity means more than just knowledge; it's about living out what we know with wisdom, love, and steadfastness, showing Christ's qualities in our words, actions, and attitudes. Spiritual maturity involves continual growth toward being "complete" or "fully developed" in Christ.

STUDY QUESTIONS

1. What does Paul mean when he says he "rejoices in what I am suffering for you" (verse 24), and how can suffering be a source of joy in the context of ministry and serving others?

_____

_____

_____

_____

2. Paul mentions the "mystery" that was hidden for ages but is now revealed (verse 26). What is this mystery, and why is it significant to Paul's ministry? Consider the meaning of "mystery" in relation to God's redemptive plan through Christ.

_____

_____

_____

_____

3. How does the phrase "Christ in you, the hope of glory" (verse 27) shape your view of your relationship with Christ and your future hope as a believer?

_____

_____

_____

_____

4. Paul's goal is to "present everyone fully mature in Christ" (verse 28). What does maturity in Christ look like, and how can you pursue this maturity in your own life?

_____

_____

_____

_____

5. In verse 29, Paul says he "strenuously contends" with all the energy Christ provides. What does this teach about the balance between personal effort and reliance on God's strength in ministry and spiritual growth?

_____

_____

_____

_____

6. How does Paul's dedication to making known the gospel and maturing others in Christ challenge or encourage you in your own approach to discipleship and sharing your faith?

_____

_____

_____

_____

STUDY SUMMARY

Colossians 1:24-29 reveals Paul's dedication to his ministry, emphasizing his willingness to endure suffering to help believers grow into full maturity in Christ. He speaks of the mystery of "Christ in you, the hope of glory," highlighting his goal to proclaim Christ and present every believer as spiritually complete through God's strength working in him.

COACHING CONNECTION

The complete coach embodies dedication, perseverance, and a commitment to fostering spiritual maturity in others. Just as Paul endures challenges to guide believers toward fullness in Christ, a coach is called to lead and inspire with patience, viewing every interaction as an opportunity to cultivate Christlike character in those they mentor.

KEYS TO WINNING

▶ VIDEO GUIDE AT KINGDOMSPORTS.ONLINE

▶ JOY IN SACRIFICIAL SERVICE

Paul rejoices in his sufferings for the sake of the church, showing that true ministry often involves personal sacrifice. This perspective encourages us to embrace challenges and sacrifices as part of serving others and advancing God's kingdom, finding joy in the impact our efforts have on others' spiritual growth.

1. How does Paul's example of rejoicing in suffering challenge your perspective on personal sacrifices and hardships you may face while serving others? Reflect on areas where you encounter difficulty or resistance in serving?

_____

_____

_____

_____

2. In what ways can you find joy in the impact your efforts have on others' spiritual growth, even when it involves personal sacrifice or inconvenience?

_____

_____

_____

_____

▶ THE MYSTERY OF "CHRIST IN YOU"

Paul speaks of the mystery revealed in the gospel: "Christ in you, the hope of glory." This profound truth reminds us that the indwelling presence of Christ brings us hope, strength, and the assurance of God's promises, empowering us to live transformed lives that reflect His glory.

1. How does the reality of "Christ in you, the hope of glory" influence the way you view your own identity and purpose?

_____

_____

_____

_____

2. In what areas of your life do you need to rely more on the strength and hope that Christ's indwelling presence provides?

_____

_____

_____

_____

▸ COMMITMENT TO SPIRITUAL MATURITY

Paul's goal is to present every believer fully mature in Christ, highlighting the importance of discipleship and growth. This takeaway challenges us to actively pursue spiritual maturity in ourselves and to help others grow in their faith, relying on God's power to guide and sustain us in this mission.

1. In what ways are you actively pursuing spiritual maturity in your own life, and what steps can you take to grow further in your faith?

_____

_____

_____

_____

2. How can you encourage and support others in their journey toward spiritual maturity, and what role does discipleship play in this commitment? How can you help others grow in their faith while relying on God's strength and wisdom?

_____

_____

_____

_____

GAME CHANGER

Colossians 1:24-29 reveals Paul's profound commitment to his ministry, even to the point of rejoicing in his sufferings for the sake of the church. Paul sees his hardships as part of God's plan to bring others to faith and growth, and he endures them willingly to help others grow spiritually. This selfless dedication calls us to reflect on our own service and to embrace sacrifice as a necessary part of serving God and others. By viewing challenges as opportunities to help others know Christ, we can find joy in the purpose our efforts bring, even when the path is difficult.

In this passage, Paul also speaks of the "mystery" revealed through the gospel: "Christ in you, the hope of glory." This truth transforms the Christian journey from mere belief to a personal, empowering relationship with Jesus. Knowing that Christ dwells within us gives us hope, strength, and purpose beyond what we could achieve on our own. It's a reminder that we are not left to grow spiritually through our own efforts but are strengthened by the presence of Christ within. Through this mystery, we find assurance that His power is at work in us, empowering us to live in ways that reflect His character.

Ultimately, Paul's goal is to "present everyone fully mature in Christ," highlighting the importance of spiritual growth and discipleship. This commitment to maturity challenges us to pursue growth actively, relying on God's power to guide and sustain us. It encourages us to invest in the spiritual growth of others, just as Paul did, by helping them to grow in knowledge, faith, and character.

ONE BIG THING

What is the most significant lesson for you to take with you from this chapter?

_____

_____

_____

_____

_____

_____

_____

_____

_____

_____

_____

_____

_____

_____

_____

_____

IMPACT PRAYER

Lord, thank You for the example of Paul's dedication in serving You, even through suffering, for the sake of others' faith and growth. Help me to embrace challenges as opportunities to share Your love and truth, finding joy in the purpose You give my efforts. Thank You for the mystery of "Christ in me, the hope of glory," and may You strengthen me in my commitment to grow and help others to mature in their walk with You, relying always on Your power to guide and sustain me. In Jesus' name, Amen.

NOTES:

★ ★ ★

CHAPTER SIX

THE COMPLETE COACH

PURSUES MATURE KNOWLEDGE

COLOSSIANS 2:1-7

STUDY STARTER

The Oakland Athletics' "Moneyball" approach is a compelling example of the power of knowledge and analytics, especially when resources are limited. In the early 2000s, General Manager Billy Beane faced the intimidating task of competing against wealthier Major League Baseball teams with far greater budgets. With one of the smallest budgets in the league, Beane and his assistant, Paul DePodesta, chose a bold and unconventional path, prioritizing data and analytics over traditional scouting methods. They focused on advanced statistics, identifying undervalued skills like on-base percentage, which provided a more accurate measure of a player's impact. This innovative emphasis on analytics enabled Beane to build a competitive team at a fraction of the cost, showing that knowledge and insight can drive success, even against seemingly impossible odds.

The Athletics' Moneyball strategy not only transformed the team's performance but also reshaped how baseball was managed across the league. As the A's achieved unexpected success, other teams took notice and began adopting similar analytical methods. Beane's knowledge-driven decisions challenged traditional baseball wisdom, but the data supported his choices, demonstrating that a foundation built on solid information could withstand scrutiny and skepticism.

Just as Beane relied on data to make informed, strategic choices, Paul urges believers to deepen their knowledge of God's Word, allowing it to guide them with wisdom and confidence. When we are "rooted and built up" in Christ, in whom are hidden all the treasures of wisdom and knowledge, we are equipped to face challenges, make wise decisions, and stay steadfast in our convictions—even when others may question our approach or tempt us with alternatives.

STUDY PASSAGE

2 *For I want you to know how great a struggle I have for you and for those at Laodicea and for all who have not seen me face to face,* [2] *that their hearts may be encouraged, being knit together in love, to reach all the riches of full assurance of understanding and the knowledge of God's mystery, which is Christ,* [3] *in whom are hidden all the treasures of wisdom and knowledge.* [4] *I say this in order that no one may delude you with plausible arguments.* [5] *For though I am absent in body, yet I am with you in spirit, rejoicing to see your good order and the firmness of your faith in Christ.* [6] *Therefore, as you received Christ Jesus the Lord, so walk in him,* [7] *rooted and built up in him and established in the faith, just as you were taught, abounding in thanksgiving. (ESV)*

STUDY HELP

- *"encouraged"*—This Greek word, often translated as "encouraged," can also mean "comforted" or "strengthened." It carries the sense of being called alongside to provide support, as a friend or advocate might. In this context, Paul's use suggests a desire for the Colossian believers to be spiritually fortified and comforted in their hearts, reflecting not only encouragement but also deep reassurance in their faith.

- *"united"*—Paul emphasizes unity as foundational for a healthy Christian community. Focusing on "united" highlights the role of love in binding believers together, creating a bond that reflects Christ's love and fosters spiritual growth.

- *"rooted"*—This term is an agricultural metaphor meaning to be deeply and securely planted. It implies permanence and stability, suggesting that believers are deeply anchored in Christ. This image helps readers see that spiritual growth depends on a firm foundation, with "roots" in Christ providing strength and resilience, much like a tree's roots stabilize it against winds and storms.

STUDY QUESTIONS

1. In verse 2, Paul says his goal is for believers to be "encouraged in heart." What does it mean to be encouraged in heart, and how can this encouragement strengthen our faith and resilience?

_____

_____

_____

_____

2. Paul speaks of being "united in love" in verse 2. How does unity in love contribute to a strong Christian community, and what role do you play in fostering this unity?

_____

_____

_____

_____

3. What is the "mystery of God" that Paul speaks of in verse 2, and why is it significant that this mystery has now been revealed in Christ?

_____

_____

_____

_____

4. In verse 3, Paul says that "all the treasures of wisdom and knowledge" are hidden in Christ. How does this affect your view of where to seek wisdom and guidance for life's challenges?

_____

_____

_____

_____

5. Paul encourages believers to be "rooted and built up in him" (verse 7). What does it mean to be rooted in Christ, and how does this foundation impact your spiritual growth and ability to withstand challenges?

_____

_____

_____

_____

6. In verse 7, Paul speaks of "overflowing with thankfulness." How does gratitude play a role in maintaining a strong faith, and how can you cultivate thankfulness in your life, especially during challenges?

_____

_____

_____

_____

STUDY SUMMARY

This passage emphasizes Paul's desire for believers to be encouraged, united in love, and rooted in Christ, where all wisdom and knowledge are found. He encourages them to remain steadfast in their faith, growing strong and overflowing with thankfulness as they build their lives on Christ.

COACHING CONNECTION

The complete coach knows the importance of encouraging others, fostering unity, and grounding one's work in Christ as the ultimate source of wisdom.

KEYS TO WINNING

▶ VIDEO GUIDE AT KINGDOMSPORTS.ONLINE

▶ THE IMPORTANCE OF ENCOURAGEMENT AND UNITY

Paul stresses the need for believers to be encouraged in heart and united in love, showing that spiritual support and unity are vital for a strong Christian community. This takeaway reminds us that mutual encouragement and love help us grow together in faith.

1. How can you actively contribute to creating a culture of encouragement and unity within your community or group, and what specific steps can you take to support others in their faith journey?

_____

_____

_____

_____

2. In what ways has mutual encouragement and love from others strengthened your own faith, and how can you share that same support with others?

_____

_____

_____

_____

▶ CHRIST AS THE SOURCE OF ALL WISDOM AND KNOWLEDGE

Paul highlights that all the treasures of wisdom and knowledge are found in Christ, emphasizing the sufficiency of Christ for understanding life's greatest questions and challenges. This encourages believers to seek wisdom in Christ, who provides true insight and guidance.

1. In what areas of your life are you seeking wisdom or guidance, and how can you intentionally turn to Christ as your primary source of insight and understanding? Reflect on how you usually approach life's questions or challenges?

_____

_____

_____

_____

2. What does it mean for you to view Christ as sufficient for life's deepest questions, and how can this belief shape your priorities and pursuits?

_____

_____

_____

_____

▸ THE NEED TO BE ROOTED AND ESTABLISHED

Paul encourages believers to be rooted, built up, and steadfast in their faith, grounded in the foundation of Christ. This image of rootedness serves as a reminder to develop a strong, resilient faith that can withstand challenges and grow through gratitude.

1. How can you deepen your roots in Christ, building a foundation to help you withstand life's challenges?

_____

_____

_____

_____

2. How does gratitude play a role in helping you grow and stay established in your faith, even during difficult times?

_____

_____

_____

_____

GAME CHANGER

In Colossians 2:1-7, Paul expresses his desire for believers to be "encouraged in heart and united in love." This encouragement and unity are not just for comfort; they are foundational for spiritual strength and growth. In our lives, encouragement from others and a sense of belonging in a faith community help us navigate challenges with resilience. Being "united in love" also reminds us that, as believers, we are interconnected, strengthening and supporting one another in our journey with Christ. Reflecting this unity, we draw closer to God and to each other, becoming a visible example of His love.

Paul then points us to Christ as the source of "all the treasures of wisdom and knowledge." This truth offers clarity and stability in a world of competing voices, guiding us to seek true wisdom and answers in Christ alone. His wisdom is sufficient for life's biggest questions, giving us a foundation we can trust and rely on. This wisdom points us back to the gospel, as Christ's life and teachings reveal God's ultimate plan for redemption and transformation. By making Christ our source of wisdom, we align our lives with His purposes, allowing His insights to shape our decisions, thoughts, and actions.

Finally, Paul encourages believers to be "rooted and built up" in Christ, reminding us that a strong faith foundation is essential for growth and resilience. Just as a tree withstands storms when firmly rooted, we can remain steadfast in difficult times when our faith is grounded in Christ. This rootedness invites us to live with gratitude, recognizing that every day, we are built up in Him, equipped to face challenges and grow deeper in our faith. Rooted in Christ and overflowing with thankfulness, we become witnesses of the gospel, showing others the strength and hope in a life built on Him.

ONE BIG THING

What is the most significant lesson for you to take with you from this chapter?

_____

_____

_____

_____

_____

_____

_____

_____

_____

_____

_____

_____

_____

_____

_____

_____

IMPACT PRAYER

Heavenly Father, thank You for the gift of encouragement and unity in Your love, which strengthens us in faith. Help us to seek all wisdom and knowledge in Christ, grounding our lives in His truth and guidance. As we root ourselves in You, may our faith grow strong and resilient, enabling us to face challenges with gratitude and hope. Let our lives be a reflection of Your love and wisdom, pointing others to the strength and peace found in You. In Jesus' name, Amen.

NOTES:

★ ★ ★

CHAPTER SEVEN

THE COMPLETE COACH

GUARDS AGAINST DECEPTION

COLOSSIANS 2:8-15

STUDY STARTER

Coach John Wooden, the legendary leader of UCLA's basketball dynasty, was known for doing more than just building winning teams—he focused on protecting his players. Wooden saw the temptation many young athletes faced to chase after shortcuts or buy into flashy gimmicks that promised instant success. With his steady, principled approach, he warned his players that true achievement couldn't be found through quick fixes or the latest trends. Instead, he taught them to rely on mastering the basics, grounding them in discipline and integrity. His famous "Pyramid of Success" was more than a motivational tool; it was a safeguard against empty promises, guiding his players to value hard work, resilience, and true growth.

Wooden's career spanned decades, and during that time, he watched as countless trends swept through the sports world, claiming to offer "the secret" to victory. He was vigilant in protecting his players from these distractions, knowing that superficial fixes could ultimately undermine their character and derail their potential. His practices were built on consistency, repetition, and a commitment to core values that didn't change with each season. Wooden knew that athletes grounded in these fundamentals would succeed on the court and be better equipped to face life's challenges. His dedication to this approach echoes Paul's warning to the Colossians in Colossians 2:8-15, where Paul cautions believers not to be "taken captive" by hollow philosophies or deceptive ideas that lead away from Christ.

Just as Wooden protected his players from shortcuts that could compromise their character, Paul urges the Colossians to remain rooted in Christ, resisting empty ideas that lack real substance. Wooden's life and teaching remind us that real success is built on a solid foundation, not fleeting trends or surface-level fixes. His legacy challenges us to focus on what's genuine and lasting and reminds us that true spiritual growth comes from grounding ourselves in the sufficiency of Christ.

STUDY PASSAGE

2 *⁸ See to it that no one takes you captive by philosophy and empty deceit, according to human tradition, according to the elemental spirits of the world, and not according to Christ. ⁹ For in him the whole fullness of deity dwells bodily, ¹⁰ and you have been filled in him, who is the head of all rule and authority. ¹¹ In him also you were circumcised with a circumcision made without hands, by putting off the body of the flesh, by the circumcision of Christ, ¹² having been buried with him in baptism, in which you were also raised with him through faith in the powerful working of God, who raised him from the dead. ¹³ And you, who were dead in your trespasses and the uncircumcision of your flesh, God made alive together with him, having forgiven us all our trespasses, ¹⁴ by canceling the record of debt that stood against us with its legal demands. This he set aside, nailing it to the cross. ¹⁵ He disarmed the rulers and authorities and put them to open shame, by triumphing over them in him. (ESV)*

STUDY HELP

- *"deception"*—This term refers to a misleading or deceptive quality, implying the allure of something false. In verse 8, Paul warns believers to be cautious of philosophies that are "hollow and deceptive," pointing to teachings that may appear attractive or wise but lack truth and substance. Paul specifically calls out human traditions and "elemental spiritual forces" (often referring to worldly or demonic influences) as sources of deception.

- *"circumcision"*—In the Old Testament, circumcision was a sign of the covenant between God and Israel, marking them as God's people. Here, Paul speaks of a spiritual circumcision—a cutting away of the sinful nature—that occurs through Christ. This spiritual circumcision signifies a new identity, setting believers apart from sin through their union with Christ.

- *"forgiven"*—This term means to "show grace" or "to forgive." Paul uses it to describe the complete forgiveness of sins given through Christ. This forgiveness isn't just transactional; it's a free gift based on God's grace, wiping out the "charge of our legal indebtedness" (verse 14). The word points to both release and pardon, symbolizing the removal of all barriers to reconciliation with God. This spiritual circumcision signifies a new identity, setting believers apart from sin through their union with Christ.

STUDY QUESTIONS

1. In verse 8, Paul warns, "See to it that no one takes you captive by philosophy and empty deceit." What does Paul mean by "empty deceit," and why is it important to guard against teachings that are "according to human tradition"? Consider current influences that may lead people away from Christ?

_____

_____

_____

_____

2. Paul writes in verse 9, "For in him the whole fullness of deity dwells bodily." How does knowing that Christ embodies the fullness of God influence your relationship with Him?

_____

_____

_____

_____

3. What does this spiritual circumcision represent, and how does it reflect the transformation that comes from being in Christ? Think about the difference between outward practices and inner spiritual change?

_____

_____

_____

_____

4. Paul says in verse 12 that we are "buried with him in baptism, in which you were also raised with him." How does this imagery of burial and resurrection illustrate the believer's new life in Christ?

_____

_____

_____

_____

5. In verse 14, Paul writes that Christ "canceled the record of debt that stood against us." What does it mean to have this record of debt canceled, and how does understanding this forgiveness affect your relationship with God?

_____

_____

_____

_____

6. Verse 15 describes Christ disarming "the rulers and authorities" and triumphing over them. How does Christ's victory over spiritual powers encourage you to rely on Him in your own struggles?

_____

_____

_____

_____

STUDY SUMMARY

Colossians 2:8-15 warns believers against being misled by deceptive philosophies and emphasizes that the fullness of God dwells in Christ, who has reconciled us through His death and resurrection. In Christ, believers are spiritually transformed, fully forgiven, and share in His victory over all spiritual powers

COACHING CONNECTION

The complete coach seeks Christ and His Word for spiritual growth, avoiding influences that distract from the gospel. They rely on the fullness, forgiveness, and victory found in Christ, helping them to lead with integrity, empower others spiritually, and stand strong against challenges in their role.

KEYS TO WINNING

▶ **VIDEO GUIDE AT KINGDOMSPORTS.ONLINE**

▶ STAY ROOTED IN CHRIST'S TRUTH

Paul warns against being taken captive by "philosophy and empty deceit," reminding believers to hold firmly to Christ's teachings and avoid worldly influences that stray from the gospel. This calls us to keep our beliefs and practices anchored in Christ alone.

1. In what areas of your life do you feel the pull of "empty deceit" or worldly influences, and how can you intentionally anchor yourself in Christ's teachings to resist these distractions?

_____

_____

_____

_____

2. How can you deepen your understanding of Christ's teachings to strengthen your foundation and help you discern between gospel truth and deceptive influences?

_____

_____

_____

_____

▶ THE FULLNESS OF GOD DWELLS IN CHRIST

Paul emphasizes that "in him the whole fullness of deity dwells bodily," affirming Christ's divinity and sufficiency. This means that believers have everything they need spiritually in Christ, who embodies the complete nature and power of God.

1. How does knowing that "the whole fullness of deity dwells bodily" in Christ impact your understanding of His power and sufficiency in your life? Reflect on what it means for Christ to embody the complete nature of God.

_____

_____

_____

_____

2. In what areas are you tempted to seek fulfillment outside of Christ, and how can recognizing His complete sufficiency help you turn back to Him as your source?

_____

_____

_____

_____

▶ CHRIST'S VICTORY AND OUR FORGIVENESS

Through Christ's death and resurrection, He has canceled our debts and triumphed over "rulers and authorities," granting us both forgiveness and freedom. This assures believers of their complete forgiveness and victory over spiritual opposition, empowering them to live confidently in God's grace.

1. How does understanding that Christ has canceled your debts and granted you complete forgiveness change the way you approach God and live out your faith daily?

_____

_____

_____

_____

2. In what areas of life do you feel spiritual opposition, and how can Christ's victory over "rulers and authorities" encourage you to face these challenges with confidence? Consider how Christ's triumph empowers you against fears or obstacles?

_____

_____

_____

_____

GAME CHANGER

Colossians 2:8-15 reminds us of the power and sufficiency of Christ, warning us not to be "taken captive by philosophy and empty deceit," which stray from the truth of the gospel. In a world full of competing ideas and beliefs, this passage calls us to remain anchored in Christ's teachings, ensuring our lives are built on His truth rather than fleeting cultural ideas. Holding firmly to Christ grounds us and protects us from the distractions and deceptions of the world. Reflecting on this warning encourages us to evaluate our lives, making sure we seek wisdom, fulfillment, and purpose in Him alone.

The passage also reveals the depth of Christ's divinity, stating that "in him the whole fullness of deity dwells bodily." This incredible truth assures us that Jesus is fully God, embodying all of God's nature and power. Knowing that we have access to the fullness of God in Christ means that we lack nothing spiritually. His presence brings all the wisdom, strength, and guidance we need. This realization points us back to the gospel—Christ is not only our Savior but our constant source, fully capable of meeting our deepest needs and guiding us through every season of life.

Ultimately, Paul's words remind us of Christ's victory and our complete forgiveness through His death and resurrection. By canceling the record of our debt, Christ has freed us from guilt and shame, and by triumphing over "rulers and authorities," He has secured victory over spiritual forces. This truth allows us to walk confidently in God's grace, empowered to live with purpose and freedom. In Christ, we are not only forgiven but are equipped to face life's challenges with the assurance that His victory is our victory.

ONE BIG THING

What is the most significant lesson for you to take with you from this chapter?

_____

_____

_____

_____

_____

_____

_____

_____

_____

_____

_____

_____

_____

_____

_____

_____

_____

_____

IMPACT PRAYER

Heavenly Father, thank You for the fullness of life and truth we have in Christ. Help us to stay rooted in Your Word, discerning truth amidst all that distracts us, and to remember that in Christ, we have everything we need. Thank You for canceling our debts and securing victory over all forces that oppose us. May we live in the freedom and confidence Your forgiveness brings, empowered by Your grace, to walk boldly and gratefully each day. In Jesus' name, Amen.

★ ★ ★

CHAPTER EIGHT
THE COMPLETE COACH

REJECTS SELF-MADE RELIGION

COLOSSIANS 2:16-23

STUDY STARTER

Coach Doc Rivers has built a successful NBA coaching career on the belief that relationships, rather than strict rules, are the foundation of a strong and unified team. When Rivers took on the head coach role for the Boston Celtics, he inherited a team of diverse personalities and strong-willed players, each with their own approach to the game. Rather than imposing rigid rules and structures, Rivers prioritized building a culture of trust and respect. He believed that players would naturally hold themselves accountable if they felt genuinely valued and connected. This approach led the Celtics to build strong chemistry and, ultimately, to an NBA Championship in 2008—a testament to Rivers' relationship-centered leadership.

Throughout his career, with teams like the LA Clippers and the Philadelphia 76ers, Rivers continued to emphasize relationships over strict rules. He gets to know his players personally, listens to their concerns, and understands their strengths. Rivers sees each player as more than a role on the court; he values their growth and well-being as individuals. Instead of setting up exhaustive rules to manage behavior, Rivers trusts that fostering mutual respect among players leads to a team that holds itself accountable. His emphasis on relational leadership has allowed him to build cohesive teams driven by a shared purpose rather than simply following a list of do's and don'ts.

Rivers' approach reflects Paul's message in Colossians 2:16-23, where Paul warns believers against relying on strict rules or "self-made religion" as a means of spirituality. Like Paul, who encourages believers to focus on their relationship with Christ rather than restrictive practices, Rivers shows that rules alone can't enforce unity and commitment. His example reminds us that genuine growth and accountability come from being grounded in relationships built on trust and respect rather than strict structures.

STUDY PASSAGE

2 [16] *Therefore let no one pass judgment on you in questions of food and drink, or with regard to a festival or a new moon or a Sabbath.* [17] *These are a shadow of the things to come, but the substance belongs to Christ.* [18] *Let no one disqualify you, insisting on asceticism and worship of angels, going on in detail about visions, puffed up without reason by his sensuous mind,* [19] *and not holding fast to the Head, from whom the whole body, nourished and knit together through its joints and ligaments, grows with a growth that is from God.* [20] *If with Christ you died to the elemental spirits of the world, why, as if you were still alive in the world, do you submit to regulations—*[21] *"Do not handle, Do not taste, Do not touch"* [22] *(referring to things that all perish as they are used)—according to human precepts and teachings?* [23] *These have indeed an appearance of wisdom in promoting self-made religion and asceticism and severity to the body, but they are of no value in stopping the indulgence of the flesh.* (ESV)

STUDY HELP

- *"judgment"*—In verse 16, Paul warns believers not to let others judge them regarding practices like dietary rules, festivals, and Sabbaths. Paul's caution suggests that such judgments were being imposed by those who still emphasized adherence to Old Testament laws or additional human traditions as necessary for spiritual maturity.

- *"shadow"*—This term refers to a "shadow" or "outline," suggesting something incomplete or insubstantial compared to the actual reality. In verse 17, Paul uses it to describe religious rituals and practices as a shadow of the true substance found in Christ. These practices pointed to God's future redemptive work but were only a temporary foreshadowing of Christ's ultimate fulfillment.

- *"asceticism"*—Although commonly translated as "asceticism," the underlying Greek term literally means "humility" or "self-abasement." In this context, it likely refers to practices of extreme self-denial, which were promoted by some as necessary for spiritual enlightenment or purity. In verse 18, Paul warns against being disqualified by those insisting on asceticism, as these practices can distract from true faith and create a false sense of superiority.

STUDY QUESTIONS

1. In verse 16, Paul says, "let no one pass judgment on you in questions of food and drink, or with regard to a festival or a new moon or a Sabbath." Why does Paul caution against judgment based on these religious practices, and how can we apply this principle today?

_____

_____

_____

_____

2. Paul describes these practices as a "shadow of the things to come" in verse 17. What does it mean that they are a shadow, and how does focusing on Christ as the substance help us understand the gospel more fully?

_____

_____

_____

_____

3. In verse 18, Paul warns against those who promote "asceticism and worship of angels." What is asceticism, and how can practices that seem spiritual distract from a true relationship with Christ?

_____

_____

_____

_____

4. Paul speaks in verse 19 of holding fast to "the Head, from whom the whole body... grows with a growth that is from God." How does being connected to Christ as the Head influence your spiritual growth and unity within the Christian community?

_____

_____

_____

_____

5. In verse 20, Paul asks why believers "submit to regulations" if they have died with Christ to the "elemental spirits of the world." How does understanding your freedom in Christ influence your approach to religious rules or external expectations?

_____

_____

_____

_____

6. Verse 23 mentions that these regulations "have an appearance of wisdom...but they are of no value in stopping the indulgence of the flesh." How can focusing on Christ rather than external rules lead to true transformation?

_____

_____

_____

_____

STUDY SUMMARY

Colossians 2:16-23 warns believers not to be judged by or bound to religious rituals, emphasizing that these practices are merely shadows of the reality found in Christ. Paul encourages believers to hold fast to Christ, the source of true spiritual growth, and to reject human regulations that appear wise but lack the power to transform the heart.

COACHING CONNECTION

The complete coach prioritizes authentic spiritual growth over rigid practices, helping others develop a faith rooted in the Word of God rather than in mere rituals or human expectations.

KEYS TO WINNING

► VIDEO GUIDE AT KINGDOMSPORTS.ONLINE

► FREEDOM FROM JUDGMENT BASED ON RITUALS

Paul encourages believers not to let others judge them regarding dietary laws, religious festivals, or the Sabbath, reminding us that Christ has freed us from being bound to these external practices. This takeaway highlights that true faith isn't about following specific rituals but about a personal, transformative relationship with Jesus through His revealed Word.

1. In what ways have you felt pressured to conform to certain practices or expectations in your faith, and how does recognizing your freedom in Christ help you focus on a more personal relationship with Him?

_____

_____

_____

_____

2. How can you prioritize a transformative relationship with Jesus over rituals or outward practices, and what changes might this bring to your daily walk with Him?

_____

_____

_____

_____

▶ CHRIST AS THE SUBSTANCE OVERSHADOWS

Religious rituals are described as a "shadow" of what's fulfilled in Christ, pointing to Him as the true reality. This encourages believers to focus on the substance—Christ Himself—rather than on practices that symbolically point to Him, deepening our understanding of faith centered in Christ.

1. In what areas of your life are you tempted to focus on outward practices or routines rather than deepening your relationship with Christ, the true substance of your faith?

_____

_____

_____

2. How does viewing Christ as the fulfillment of all spiritual practices and symbols change how you understand and approach your faith?

_____

_____

_____

▶ TRUTH MATURITY COMES FROM HOLDING FAST TO CHRIST

Paul stresses that spiritual growth and strength come from being connected to Christ, the Head of the body. This teaches us that authentic transformation isn't found in external regulations but in a deep, reliant relationship with Christ, who provides the growth that is from God.

1. In what ways are you currently relying on external practices or personal efforts for spiritual growth, and how can you shift to a deeper dependence on Christ as the true source of maturity?

_____

_____

_____

_____

2. Consider what it means to grow by relying on Christ rather than on external rules. How can you prioritize this connection with Christ in your daily life to experience authentic growth, and how is it connected to knowing His Word?

_____

_____

_____

_____

GAME CHANGER

In this text, Paul addresses the pressures of religious judgment and ritual, encouraging believers not to let others "pass judgment" on them based on outward practices like dietary laws or religious festivals. This passage brings tremendous relief for those struggling to measure up to external expectations. Paul's message reminds us that our faith is not about strict adherence to rituals but our freedom in Christ. This freedom shifts our focus from gaining approval through practices to building a genuine relationship with

Jesus. Recognizing this truth helps us let go of comparison and judgment, finding rest in the acceptance that Christ has already given us.

Paul describes these religious observances as a "shadow" of things to come, with Christ being the true substance. This powerful metaphor illustrates that rituals were always meant to point us toward the fullness found in Jesus. When we focus on Christ as the center, our faith becomes more than a set of rules; it becomes a relationship grounded in Him and His Word. Christ fulfills every need that rituals only symbolized, giving us direct access to God through His sacrifice. This reminder points us back to the gospel, the good news that Christ alone is sufficient and that we have everything we need in Him for a vibrant, growing faith.

Ultimately, Paul urges believers to hold fast to Christ, who is the Head of the body and the source of true growth. Spiritual maturity comes not from following rules but from staying connected to Christ. His presence provides the strength and guidance that leads to authentic transformation. This passage calls us to pursue a deeper, more reliant relationship with Christ, trusting that He will shape and grow us from within. In Christ, we find the freedom, fulfillment, and growth we need—gifts that flow from His grace rather than our own efforts.

ONE BIG THING

What is the most significant lesson from this chapter for you to take with you?

_____

_____

_____

_____

_____

_____

_____

_____

IMPACT PRAYER

Lord, thank You for the freedom and fullness we have in Christ, who has freed us from the burden of trying to earn approval through rituals. Help us to center our lives on Him, the true substance of our faith, and let go of anything that distracts us from a genuine relationship with You. Teach us to hold fast to Christ each day, relying on His presence for real transformation and growth. May our lives reflect the beauty of the gospel, living not by rules but by the grace and strength that come from knowing Him. In Jesus' name, Amen.

★ ★ ★

CHAPTER NINE
THE COMPLETE COACH
PUTS OFF THE OLD MAN

COLOSSIANS 3:1-11

STUDY STARTER

When Bill Snyder took over as head coach of Kansas State University's football program in 1989, he faced what many called an impossible task. The team was regarded as one of the worst in college football history, with a culture of losing so ingrained that players, fans, and even the school had come to expect failure. Snyder knew that to turn the program around, he had to do more than change playbooks; he needed to overhaul the entire mindset of everyone involved. This meant "putting off" the old ways of doing things—the attitudes of defeat, the lack of accountability, and the tendency to accept mediocrity—and replacing them with a new vision focused on discipline, responsibility, and the possibility of success.

Snyder introduced a philosophy called "Commitment to Excellence," which became the cornerstone of the team's transformation. Every player was held to high standards, not just in their athletic performance but also in their character and effort. Snyder emphasized personal responsibility, requiring each player to put in the hard work needed to improve individually and as a team. He didn't tolerate negativity or laziness, encouraging players to shed any attitudes that held them back. This shift in approach demanded that players set aside their old mentality and embrace a winning culture, one that was built on hard work, unity, and a belief in the value of each practice, each play, and each game. Over time, Snyder's focus on these new values took root, and the team began to see real progress.

Paul urges believers in Colossians 3:1-1 to "put off" the old self and embrace their new life rooted in Christ. Just as Snyder challenged his team to reject the defeatist mindset and adopt a culture of excellence, Paul calls believers to let go of worldly attitudes and behaviors that hinder their growth and success in their battle against sin. Lasting change begins when we put off the destructive ways of the world and set our minds on things above.

STUDY PASSAGE

3 *If then you have been raised with Christ, seek the things that are above, where Christ is, seated at the right hand of God. ² Set your minds on things that are above, not on things that are on earth. ³ For you have died, and your life is hidden with Christ in God. ⁴ When Christ who is your life appears, then you also will appear with him in glory.*

⁵ Put to death therefore what is earthly in you: sexual immorality, impurity, passion, evil desire, and covetousness, which is idolatry. ⁶ On account of these the wrath of God is coming. ⁷ In these you too once walked, when you were living in them. ⁸ But now you must put them all away: anger, wrath, malice, slander, and obscene talk from your mouth. ⁹ Do not lie to one another, seeing that you have put off the old self with its practices ¹⁰ and have put on the new self, which is being renewed in knowledge after the image of its creator. ¹¹ Here there is not Greek and Jew, circumcised and uncircumcised, barbarian, Scythian, slave, free; but Christ is all, and in all. (ESV)

STUDY HELP

- *"seek"* – In verse 1, Paul calls believers to "seek the things that are above," suggesting a purposeful pursuit of heavenly values and priorities. This verb indicates that seeking is more than a passive wish; it's an active, ongoing pursuit of God's will, reflecting a heart and mind set on spiritual things.

- *"put to death"* – The Greek term for "put to death," is a strong word that literally means "to make dead" or "to render powerless." In verse 5, Paul commands believers to "put to death" sinful behaviors and desires associated with earthly living. This language is intentional, portraying sin as something that must be decisively and permanently renounced.

- *"renewed"* – In verse 10, Paul describes the "new self" as "being renewed in knowledge after the image of its creator." This renewal is not a one-time event but a continuous spiritual transformation as believers grow in their understanding of and relationship with God. It implies a dynamic process where believers are progressively restored to reflect God's image.

STUDY QUESTIONS

1. In verse 1, Paul encourages believers to "seek the things that are above." What does it mean to actively seek heavenly things, and how can this pursuit shape your daily priorities?

_____

_____

_____

_____

2. Verse 2 says to "set your minds on things that are above, not on things that are on earth." How does adopting a heavenly mindset influence the way you view and respond to worldly matters?

_____

_____

_____

_____

3. Paul instructs believers in verse 5 to "put to death" earthly behaviors. What does it mean to put sin to death, and why is this a crucial step in the believer's life?

_____

_____

_____

_____

4. In verse 9, Paul calls believers to "put off the old self with its practices." What does the "old self" represent, and how can you identify and discard old habits that don't align with your identity in Christ?

_____

_____

_____

_____

5. Verse 10 speaks of the "new self, which is being renewed in knowledge after the image of its creator." How does growing in the knowledge of God contribute to your spiritual renewal and transformation?

_____

_____

_____

_____

6. In verse 11, Paul emphasizes unity in Christ, saying there is no "Greek and Jew, circumcised and uncircumcised" in the new self. How does this new identity in Christ promote unity?

_____

_____

_____

_____

STUDY SUMMARY

Colossians 3:1-11 calls believers to set their minds on heavenly things, shedding old sinful habits and embracing a new identity in Christ. Paul emphasizes transformation through spiritual renewal, urging believers to live in unity, reflecting the image of Christ in all they do.

COACHING CONNECTION

The complete coach sets the example by focusing on Christ-centered values, discarding harmful, sinful habits, and embracing a renewed identity in Christ.

KEYS TO WINNING

▶ **VIDEO GUIDE AT KINGDOMSPORTS.ONLINE**

▶ FOCUS ON HEAVENLY PRIORITIES

Paul urges believers to "seek the things that are above" and "set your minds on things that are above," emphasizing the importance of focusing on God's values rather than earthly distractions. This encourages believers to prioritize a mindset and lifestyle that reflects their identity in Christ.

1. How can you incorporate regular confession and repentance into your life, and what impact do you believe this will have on your relationship with God and others?

_____

_____

_____

_____

2. Reflecting on the Israelites' public confession, how can you foster a culture of openness and accountability within your community or church to encourage repentance (James 5:16)?

_____

_____

_____

_____

▶ PUT OFF THE OLD SELF

Paul calls for believers to "put to death" earthly, sinful behaviors, showing that true transformation involves decisively rejecting past habits and actions that conflict with a life in Christ. This takeaway highlights the importance of actively resisting sin as part of spiritual growth.

1. What old habits or behaviors in your life conflict with your new identity in Christ, and how can you take intentional steps to "put them to death" with God's help?

_____

_____

_____

_____

2. How does viewing transformation as an ongoing process of actively rejecting sin change your approach to spiritual growth?

_____

_____

_____

_____

▶ EMBRACE UNITY AND RENEWAL IN CHRIST

In the "new self," there is no division, and believers are "being renewed in knowledge after the image of its creator." This emphasizes that the new identity in Christ promotes unity across differences and invites ongoing spiritual renewal, encouraging believers to reflect God's image together.

1. How can you actively contribute to unity within your church, setting aside differences to reflect the new identity you share in Christ?

_____

_____

_____

_____

2. How does understanding renewal as an ongoing process inspire you to seek growth and knowledge in your relationship with God daily?

_____

_____

_____

_____

GAME CHANGER

Colossians 3:1-11 calls believers to a new way of life, rooted in Christ and focused on heavenly priorities. Paul urges us to "seek the things that are above" and to set our minds on what is eternal, not on earthly distractions. This shift in focus challenges us to reevaluate our goals, desires, and daily choices, prioritizing God's values over worldly pursuits. Keeping our thoughts and hearts aligned with Christ reminds us that our true identity and purpose are found in Him. This call to seek the things above isn't just about an occasional thought—it's about a consistent, intentional pursuit of Christ that reshapes our lives.

Paul emphasizes the importance of "putting to death" the old self, which includes earthly behaviors and attitudes that hinder our growth in Christ. The gospel invites us into true transformation, but it also requires us to consciously choose to reject patterns of sin. As we grow in our faith, we're called to let go of habits, mindsets, and reactions that don't reflect the character of Christ. This is a powerful reminder that spiritual growth is active; it's about taking steps to resist sin daily, leaning on God's strength to make real changes in our lives.

Finally, Colossians 3:1-11 reminds us that, in Christ, we are part of a unified and continually renewing body of believers. In this new identity, divisions fade, and we are being renewed "in knowledge after the image of its creator." This means that our journey in Christ is one of continuous growth, shaped by His truth and empowered by His grace. Through this renewal, we become more like Christ, reflecting His love and unity with others. This passage points us back to the gospel's transformative power, calling us to live out our faith with purpose, allowing Christ's presence within us to shine for others.

ONE BIG THING

What is the most significant lesson for you to take with you from this chapter?

_____

_____

_____

_____

_____

_____

_____

_____

_____

_____

IMPACT PRAYER

Lord, thank You for our new life in Christ and the invitation to seek what is above, focusing our hearts on You. Help us to let go of old patterns that keep us from growing, giving us the strength to put to death anything that hinders our walk with You. Renew us daily in Your image, filling us with a spirit of unity and purpose so we may reflect Your love and grace in all we do. In Jesus' name, Amen.

NOTES:

★ ★ ★

CHAPTER TEN

THE COMPLETE COACH

PUTS ON THE NEW MAN

COLOSSIANS 3:12-16

STUDY STARTER

When PJ Fleck became the head coach of the University of Minnesota football team in 2017, he knew that turning the program around required more than new plays or strategies; it needed a new culture. The team had endured years of inconsistent performance, and Fleck recognized that his players needed a fresh, unified perspective. He introduced his "Row the Boat" philosophy, a mantra that embodies resilience, teamwork, and an unwavering commitment to progress. Fleck emphasized that success would only come if every player embraced a positive mindset, worked together selflessly, and focused on continual growth. His goal was to replace the old, fragmented culture with a united attitude grounded in trust and accountability.

Fleck encouraged his players to "put on" values that would build a winning culture—values like humility, gratitude, and discipline. He taught them that "Row the Boat" wasn't just about showing up for practice but about choosing resilience and determination every day, even off the field. Fleck fostered a family-like environment where teammates supported one another, celebrated each other's growth, and worked towards shared goals. This approach shifted the atmosphere of the program, creating a strong bond among the players. Fleck emphasized that each player had a role in contributing to the team's success, and by "putting on" values of unity and dedication, the Gophers transformed from a struggling program into a competitive force.

Fleck's approach to building a new team culture mirrors Paul's instruction in Colossians 3:12-16, where believers are not only called to "put off" negative behaviors but also to actively "put on" virtues like compassion, kindness, humility, and patience. Paul recognizes that transformation requires more than just shedding sinful attitudes and habits; it calls for replacing them with Christ-like qualities. In a similar way, Fleck's "Row the Boat" mentality emphasizes the need to replace the old attitudes of defeat and division with a mindset of selflessness, resilience, and mutual support. He understood that if his players were only told what not to do, they would remain disconnected and unsure of how to move forward; they needed a positive framework to guide them.

STUDY PASSAGE

3 *¹² Put on then, as God's chosen ones, holy and beloved, compassionate hearts, kindness, humility, meekness, and patience, ¹³ bearing with one another and, if one has a complaint against another, forgiving each other; as the Lord has forgiven you, so you also must forgive. ¹⁴ And above all these put on love, which binds everything together in perfect harmony. ¹⁵ And let the peace of Christ rule in your hearts, to which indeed you were called in one body. And be thankful. ¹⁶ Let the word of Christ dwell in you richly, teaching and admonishing one another in all wisdom, singing psalms and hymns and spiritual songs, with thankfulness in your hearts to God. (ESV)*

STUDY HELP

- *"compassionate hearts"*—This word suggests a deep, heartfelt empathy that moves one to care for others with sensitivity and kindness. It implies a readiness to be emotionally invested in the lives of others, particularly in their suffering, and is often associated with God's merciful nature. In the cultural context, compassion reflects the care that God shows toward humanity, calling believers to imitate His kindness.

- *"love"*—This is the Greek word for selfless, sacrificial love, which seeks the highest good of others without expecting anything in return. In verse 14, Paul calls love the binding force that holds all virtues together "in perfect harmony." This suggests that love is foundational—it integrates other virtues and creates a unity that cannot be achieved through mere obligation. Love here is active and transformational, reflecting God's unconditional love toward us.

- *"thankful"*—This word implies an attitude of gratitude rooted in an awareness of God's grace and blessings. In the context of verse 15, Paul's command to "be thankful" reflects an inner posture that acknowledges God's goodness regardless of circumstances, encouraging believers to cultivate joy and peace by focusing on God's work in their lives.

STUDY QUESTIONS

1. In verse 12, Paul urges believers to "put on" qualities like compassion, kindness, humility, meekness, and patience. What does it mean to "put on" these virtues, and how can you practice embodying them in your daily life?

_____

_____

_____

_____

2. Verse 13 calls us to forgive others as the Lord has forgiven us. How does understanding Christ's forgiveness toward you shape the way you approach forgiveness in your own life?

_____

_____

_____

_____

3. Paul says in verse 14, "above all these put on love." Why does Paul place such a high priority on love, and how does love bind all other virtues together in harmony?

_____

_____

_____

_____

4. In verse 15, Paul encourages believers to "let the peace of Christ rule in your hearts." What does it mean for Christ's peace to "rule" in your heart, and how can you cultivate this peace amid daily challenges?

_____

_____

_____

_____

5. Paul emphasizes thankfulness in verse 15, saying, "And be thankful." How does a spirit of gratitude impact your outlook on life and your interactions with others?

_____

_____

_____

_____

6. Verse 16 calls believers to "let the word of Christ dwell in you richly." How can immersing yourself in God's Word influence your spiritual growth and the way you teach and encourage others?

_____

_____

_____

_____

STUDY SUMMARY

Colossians 3:12-16 calls believers to embody Christlike virtues—compassion, kindness, humility, forgiveness, and love—while allowing the peace of Christ and gratitude to guide their hearts. Paul emphasizes the importance of letting God's Word dwell richly within, shaping our interactions and building a unified, spiritually grounded community.

COACHING CONNECTION

The complete coach leads with Christlike qualities such as compassion, patience, and love, fostering a spirit of unity and gratitude, and understands the importance of not only telling players what not to do but that it is just as important to tell them what they should be doing.

KEYS TO WINNING

▶ VIDEO GUIDE AT KINGDOMSPORTS.ONLINE

▶ EMBRACE CHRISTLIKE VIRTUES

Paul calls believers to "put on" qualities like compassion, kindness, humility, meekness, and patience, reflecting Christ's character. This emphasizes the importance of actively embodying these virtues in our relationships, helping to build a loving and supportive community.

1. Which virtues—compassion, kindness, humility, meekness, or patience—do you find most challenging to embody, and what steps can you take to actively grow in this area?

_____

_____

_____

_____

2. How does intentionally "putting on" these virtues change how you interact with others, especially in difficult situations? How does it contrast to "putting off," and why is it important to do both?

_____

_____

_____

_____

▶ PRIORITIZE LOVE AND FORGIVENESS

Paul highlights love as the virtue that binds all others in harmony and calls believers to forgive as Christ forgave them. This shows that love and forgiveness are foundational for unity and peace within the body of Christ and foster healthy, grace-filled relationships.

1. How can you practice a deeper, Christlike love that brings unity to your relationships, especially in moments of tension or disagreement?

_____

_____

_____

_____

2. How does reflecting on Christ's forgiveness toward you impact your willingness to forgive others, even when it's difficult?

_____

_____

_____

_____

▶ CULTIVATE GRATITUDE AND THE PEACE OF CHRIST

By encouraging gratitude and allowing the peace of Christ to rule in our hearts, Paul shows how these attitudes shape our mindset and interactions. Living with thankfulness and inner peace helps believers remain grounded in their faith, even amidst challenges.

1. How can you make gratitude a daily practice that influences your perspective, even during difficult times?

_____

_____

_____

_____

2. What steps can you take to let the peace of Christ "rule in your heart," especially when facing stress or conflict?

_____

_____

_____

_____

GAME CHANGER

Colossians 3:12-16 calls us to embody qualities that reflect Christ—compassion, kindness, humility, meekness, and patience—not only as virtues to avoid the negative but as positive attributes we actively pursue. Paul describes these virtues as garments to "put on" as God's chosen people, holy and beloved. This imagery invites us to purposefully clothe ourselves with these qualities, treating others with grace even in challenging situations. These virtues become more than occasional responses; they reflect a continual transformation rooted in our identity in Christ. When we choose to act with compassion and kindness, we show others a tangible expression of God's love and model what it means to be truly valued and cared for.

The passage further underscores the importance of love and forgiveness, describing love as the unifying virtue that binds all others in harmony. Paul's instruction to "forgive as the Lord forgave you" serves as a reminder of the grace extended to us through Christ's sacrifice. This grace releases us from condemnation and calls us to restore relationships with others. Forgiveness becomes an act of imitating Christ, breaking cycles of bitterness, and fostering healing. By embracing both love and forgiveness, we cultivate a community where grace flows freely, encouraging reconciliation and unity.

Paul also urges us to "let the peace of Christ rule in your hearts" and to embrace a spirit of thankfulness. This peace, grounded in our security in Christ, enables us to face life's challenges with calm assurance. Likewise, gratitude helps us recognize God's ongoing goodness, anchoring us in His faithfulness. By letting Christ's peace guide us and practicing gratitude, we become testimonies of the gospel's transformative power, radiating joy and stability that draw others to God's love. Through these virtues, we don't just avoid negative behaviors; we positively the qualities of Christlikeness, pointing others to the hope and love found in Him.

ONE BIG THING

What is the most significant lesson for you to take with you from this chapter?

_____

_____

_____

_____

_____

_____

_____

_____

_____

_____

_____

_____

_____

_____

_____

_____

_____

IMPACT PRAYER

Heavenly Father, grant us the grace to put on these virtues each day, forgiving as You have forgiven us and letting Your peace rule in our hearts. Teach us to live in gratitude, seeing Your blessings in every circumstance, and to create harmony in our relationships through Your love. May our lives be a testimony of the life-changing grace. In Jesus' name, Amen.

NOTES:

★ ★ ★

CHAPTER ELEVEN
THE COMPLETE COACH

SERVES CHRIST IN EVERYTHING

COLOSSIANS 3:17-4:1

STUDY STARTER

Coach Mike Tomlin, head coach of the Pittsburgh Steelers, built a career and a team culture around the priority of serving one another in everything. Known for his intense dedication and high standards, Tomlin emphasizes to his players that true greatness isn't just about individual success but about uplifting and supporting those around them. He instills a "next man up" mentality, where each player is prepared to step in and serve the team at any moment, ready to fill the needs of others without hesitation. This philosophy ensures that every player feels valued and respected, creating a sense of shared responsibility and mutual support that strengthens the team.

Tomlin often reminds his players that their actions, whether on the field, in the locker room, or in their personal lives, affect the whole team. He encourages veterans to mentor younger players, teaching them not only the skills of the game but also the values of discipline, resilience, and integrity. This emphasis on serving each other builds a strong bond among players, who see themselves as athletes and as part of a family with a purpose beyond the scoreboard. Tomlin's players know they are expected to show up for one another—whether that means stepping up in a challenging game or offering encouragement during tough times. His commitment to a culture of service has created a team that thrives on mutual respect and accountability.

In Colossians 3, Paul encourages believers to do everything, "whether in word or deed," in the name of the Lord, treating others with love, respect, and humility. Paul urges Christians to serve wholeheartedly, finding true success not in personal gain but in lifting one another up. This principle reminds us that serving one another in any community—a church, a family, or a team—creates a foundation of unity and purpose. When we prioritize serving others and approach every action with humility, we honor God and build a culture where support and strength flourish.

STUDY PASSAGE

3 *17 And whatever you do, in word or deed, do everything in the name of the Lord Jesus, giving thanks to God the Father through him. 18 Wives, submit to your husbands, as is fitting in the Lord. 19 Husbands, love your wives, and do not be harsh with them. 20 Children, obey your parents in everything, for this pleases the Lord. 21 Fathers, do not provoke your children, lest they become discouraged. 22 Bondservants, obey in everything those who are your earthly masters, not by way of eye-service, as people-pleasers, but with sincerity of heart, fearing the Lord. 23 Whatever you do, work heartily, as for the Lord and not for men, 24 knowing that from the Lord you will receive the inheritance as your reward. You are serving the Lord Christ. 25 For the wrongdoer will be paid back for the wrong he has done, and there is no partiality.*

4 *Masters, treat your bondservants justly and fairly, knowing that you also have a Master in heaven. (ESV)*

STUDY HELP

- *"word and deed"*—In verse 17, Paul includes "word" alongside "deed" to show that everything a believer says should align with the character of Christ. Logos in this context emphasizes the power and responsibility of our speech, reminding believers that their words reflect their faith and commitment to Jesus.

- *"household code"*—The "household code" in Colossians 3:18-4:1 is a set of instructions Paul provides for the Christian household, covering relationships between husbands and wives, parents and children, and masters and servants. This code outlines specific behaviors and attitudes that promote harmony, respect, and Christ-centered living within the family and household structure. Rather than reflecting the authoritarian structures typical of the Greco-Roman culture, Paul's instructions are rooted in mutual respect and responsibility, with each role guided by a commitment to Christ and His teachings.

- *"work heartily"*—This phrase indicates that believers should approach their work with full dedication, not just performing tasks for human approval but as an act of worship for God. This understanding elevates all forms of work—whether mundane or significant—to an offering for God, done with sincerity, integrity, and purpose.

STUDY QUESTIONS

1. In Colossians 3:17, Paul says to do everything "in the name of the Lord Jesus." What does it mean to live in a way that represents Jesus in both "word and deed," and how can this influence your everyday actions?

_____

_____

_____

_____

2. In verse 18, Paul instructs wives to submit to their husbands "as is fitting in the Lord." What does submission mean within marriage?

_____

_____

_____

_____

3. Verse 19 calls on husbands to love their wives and "not be harsh with them." What does it teach about the Christlike approach to leadership?

_____

_____

_____

_____

4. In verse 20, Paul encourages children to obey their parents "in everything." Why is obedience important in the family context, and how does it contribute to a respectful and harmonious household?

_____

_____

_____

_____

5. Verse 21 cautions fathers not to provoke their children "lest they become discouraged." Why must parents, especially fathers, guide their children with gentleness, and how can this approach impact their spiritual development?

_____

_____

_____

_____

6. In verses 22-23, Paul instructs servants to obey their earthly masters "with sincerity of heart" and to "work heartily, as for the Lord." How does this guidance apply to modern work relationships, and how can believers embody these principles in their jobs today?

_____

_____

_____

_____

STUDY SUMMARY

Colossians 3:17-4:1 instructs believers to live in a way that reflects Christ's character in every word and deed, promoting humility, love, and respect within family and work relationships. Paul emphasizes that, whether leading or serving, all should act with integrity and justice, knowing they are accountable to Christ, the ultimate Master.

COACHING CONNECTION

The complete coach models Christlike character in every interaction, demonstrating humility, respect, and integrity, always mindful of their ultimate accountability to Christ as the true Master.

KEYS TO WINNING

▶ **VIDEO GUIDE AT KINGDOMSPORTS.ONLINE**

▶ LIVE FOR CHRIST IN EVERY WORD AND DEED

Paul calls believers to do everything "in the name of the Lord Jesus," which means that their speech and actions should reflect Christ's character. This message reminds us that all aspects of life—home, work, or public—are opportunities to honor Christ.

1. In what areas of your life do you find it challenging to reflect Christ's character, and how can you intentionally invite Him into these areas to honor Him through your words and actions?

_____

_____

_____

_____

2. How can you make "doing everything in the name of the Lord Jesus" a daily mindset that guides your interactions, decisions, and responsibilities?

_____

_____

_____

_____

▶ PRACTICE HUMILITY, LOVE, AND INTEGRITY IN RELATIONSHIPS

Paul's instructions for family and work relationships emphasize mutual respect, compassion, and just treatment, showing that Christlike love should shape every relationship. Everyone is encouraged to act with integrity and humility, whether leading or following.

1. How can you show greater humility and compassion in your interactions with others, especially those who may be difficult to love or respect?

_____

_____

_____

_____

2. How does acting with integrity impact the trust and respect within your relationships, and what steps can you take to ensure that your actions consistently align with your values?

_____

_____

_____

_____

▶ REMEMBER ACCOUNTABILITY TO CHRIST

For those in positions of authority, Paul's reminder that Christ is the ultimate Master calls for leadership marked by fairness and justice. This takeaway encourages us to lead with a sense of responsibility, knowing we answer to God for how we treat others.

1. How does knowing you are accountable to Christ influence how you lead and make decisions, especially when facing pressures or challenges in your role?

_____

_____

_____

_____

2. In what areas of leadership can you improve your ability to treat others fairly and respectfully, knowing that Christ values and observes each interaction?

_____

_____

_____

_____

GAME CHANGER

This section challenges us to live purposefully, dedicating every word and deed to Christ. Paul calls us to represent Jesus in what we do and how we do it, whether at home, in relationships, or in the workplace. This passage reminds us that every aspect of our lives is an opportunity to honor Christ, making our everyday routines reflect His character. When we approach each task and interaction with this mindset, even ordinary moments become acts of worship that deepen our faith and point others to Jesus.

Paul emphasizes the importance of humility, love, and integrity. He calls us to lead and serve with compassion, treating others with respect and fairness, whether in a position of authority or following someone else's lead. This Christlike approach to relationships fosters an environment of grace, harmony, and mutual support, mirroring God's love in practical ways. By choosing humility and kindness, we create spaces where people feel valued, respected, and loved, embodying the heart of the gospel.

Paul's reminder that Christ is the ultimate Master gives us a perspective that transforms how we view authority and accountability. In all our roles, we ultimately serve Christ, answering to Him for our actions and how we treat others. This sense of accountability inspires us to lead with justice and compassion, aware that our actions have eternal significance. Embracing this call to live in integrity and love, we become witnesses of the gospel, showing that a life rooted in Christ's character can bring light, hope, and transformation to those around us.

ONE BIG THING

What is the most significant lesson for you to take with you from this chapter?

_____

_____

_____

_____

_____

_____

_____

_____

_____

_____

_____

_____

_____

_____

_____

_____

_____

_____

IMPACT PRAYER

Heavenly Father, we desire to honor You in every facet of our lives. Empower us to commit each word we speak and every action we take to glorify Your name. Fill our relationships with humility, love, and integrity, reflecting Your character to those around us. Remind us that we are accountable to You above all, and guide us to lead with compassion and fairness. In Jesus' name, Amen.

★ ★ ★

CHAPTER TWELVE
THE COMPLETE COACH
STRIVES FOR WISDOM

COLOSSIANS 4:2-18

STUDY STARTER

Scott Drew, head basketball coach at Baylor University, built his program on a foundation emphasizing growth in every area of life. Drew's approach to coaching goes beyond wins and losses; he sees basketball as an opportunity to help young men grow in integrity, purpose, and faith. In his book, *The Road to J.O.Y.: Leading with Faith, Playing with Purpose, Leaving a Legacy,* Drew explains his "J.O.Y." philosophy, which prioritizes Jesus first, then Others, then Yourself. This approach underscores his belief that true success is not just about personal achievements but a life oriented toward Christ and serving others.

Drew's commitment to holistic growth is evident in his everyday interactions with his players. As he leads them on and off the court, he encourages them to excel academically, build strong relationships, and grow spiritually. Drew's influence has helped transform Baylor into a national powerhouse. Yet, he remains devoted to the mission of fostering each player's character, knowing that their faith journey is ultimately more impactful than any championship.

In Colossians 4:2-18, Paul urges believers to "devote themselves to prayer," being "watchful and thankful" (Colossians 4:2), and to live in a way that honors Christ in every area of life. He emphasizes the importance of making the most of every opportunity, speaking and acting with wisdom, grace, and integrity (Colossians 4:5-6). Paul suggests maturity is about becoming well-rounded in Christ—rooted in love, purpose, and wisdom, and actively serving others. Scott Drew, through his holistic approach to coaching, reflects this call by emphasizing character, faith, and service alongside athletic development.

STUDY PASSAGE

4 *² Continue steadfastly in prayer, being watchful in it with thanksgiving. ³ At the same time, pray also for us, that God may open to us a door for the word, to declare the mystery of Christ, on account of which I am in prison—⁴ that I may make it clear, which is how I ought to speak. ⁵ Walk in wisdom toward outsiders, making the best use of the time. ⁶ Let your speech always be gracious, seasoned with salt, so that you may know how you ought to answer each person. ⁷ Tychicus will tell you all about my activities. He is a beloved brother and faithful minister and fellow servant in the Lord. ⁸ I have sent him to you for this very purpose, that you may know how we are and that he may encourage your hearts, ⁹ and with him Onesimus, our faithful and beloved brother, who is one of you. They will tell you of everything that has taken place here. ¹⁰ Aristarchus my fellow prisoner greets you, and Mark the cousin of Barnabas (concerning whom you have received instructions—if he comes to you, welcome him), ¹¹ and Jesus who is called Justus. These are the only men of the circumcision among my fellow workers for the kingdom of God, and they have been a comfort to me. ¹² Epaphras, who is one of you, a servant of Christ Jesus, greets you, always struggling on your behalf in his prayers, that you may stand mature and fully assured in all the will of God. ¹³ For I bear him witness that he has worked hard for you and for those in Laodicea and in Hierapolis. ¹⁴ Luke the beloved physician greets you, as does Demas. ¹⁵ Give my greetings to the brothers at Laodicea, and to Nympha and the church in her house. ¹⁶ And when this letter has been read among you, have it also read in the church of the Laodiceans; and see that you also read the letter from Laodicea. ¹⁷ And say to Archippus, "See that you fulfill the ministry that you have received in the Lord." ¹⁸ I, Paul, write this greeting with my own hand. Remember my chains. Grace be with you. (ESV)*

STUDY HELP

- *"prayer"*—In Colossians 4:2, Paul exhorts the believers to "continue steadfastly in prayer," emphasizing persistence and dedication in their prayer life. The phrase "being watchful in it with thanksgiving" adds layers to the concept of prayer, combining alertness with gratitude.

- *"best use of time"*—This term carries the idea of purchasing something completely or reclaiming it, specifically in this case, time. Sometimes translated as "redeeming the time," it suggests actively seizing every favorable moment to reflect Christ and advance the gospel. Time is a valuable commodity that can be "bought back" or rescued from being wasted.

- *"seasoned with salt"*—In ancient times, salt was valuable for preserving qualities and enhancing flavor. In Colossians 4:6, Paul uses this metaphor to describe how believers' speech should be engaging, pure, and preserving the truth. These rituals underscored the importance of holiness and cleanliness in approaching God, symbolizing the removal of sin and the restoration of a right relationship with Him.

STUDY QUESTIONS

1. In verse 2, Paul encourages believers to "continue steadfastly in prayer." What does it mean to be persistent and watchful in prayer, and how can you incorporate thanksgiving into your prayer life?

_____

_____

_____

_____

2. Paul asks for prayer that God would "open a door for the word" (verse 3). How does this show Paul's dependence on God for opportunities to share the gospel, and how can you apply this dependence in your own life?

_____

_____

_____

_____

3. In verse 5, Paul calls believers to "walk in wisdom toward outsiders." What does it look like to walk in wisdom, especially when interacting with those who may not share your beliefs?

_____

_____

_____

_____

4. The phrase "redeeming the time" in verse 5 suggests using every opportunity wisely. What does it mean to redeem the time, and how can you ensure that your daily life reflects this principle?

_____

_____

_____

_____

5. In verse 6, Paul encourages believers to let their speech be "gracious, seasoned with salt." How can gracious and thoughtful speech help you represent Christ in your interactions?

_____

_____

_____

_____

6. Verses 7-18 include Paul's final greetings, acknowledging his team members and fellow workers. What do these personal greetings reveal about the importance of community and partnership in ministry?

_____

_____

_____

_____

STUDY SUMMARY

Colossians 4:2-18 encourages believers to be devoted in prayer, wise in their interactions, and intentional in their speech, making the most of every opportunity to represent Christ. Paul's final greetings emphasize the importance of community and partnership in ministry, showing how mutual support strengthens the work of the gospel.

COACHING CONNECTION

The complete coach embraces steadfast prayer, wise interactions, and intentional speech, using every opportunity to reflect Christ's character.

KEYS TO WINNING

▶ VIDEO GUIDE AT KINGDOMSPORTS.ONLINE

▶ BE DEVOTED IN PRAYER WITH GRATITUDE

Paul encourages believers to remain steadfast in prayer, watching and giving thanks. This highlights the importance of maintaining a close, thankful relationship with God, relying on Him for guidance and strength.

1. In what areas of your life do you struggle with maintaining steadfast prayer, and how can incorporating gratitude help you deepen your connection with God in those areas?

_____

_____

_____

_____

2. How does regularly giving thanks in prayer shift your perspective on life's challenges and remind you of God's faithfulness?

_____

_____

_____

_____

▶ MAKE THE MOST OF EVERY OPPORTUNITY

Paul calls believers to "walk in wisdom" and "redeem the time," emphasizing intentionality in how we interact with others, especially non-believers. This encourages believers to actively seek ways to share their faith and to be mindful of the impact of their words and actions.

1. How can you become more intentional about using everyday interactions as opportunities to reflect Christ's love, especially with those who may not share your beliefs?

_____

_____

_____

_____

2. In what areas of your life might you be overlooking opportunities to share your faith, and how can you start to redeem the time in those moments?

_____

_____

_____

_____

▶ VALUE COMMUNITY AND PARTNERSHIP

Paul demonstrates the importance of community and mutual support in ministry through his final greetings. His acknowledgment of fellow workers shows that the work of the gospel is strengthened by collaboration, encouragement, and shared purpose among believers.

1. How can you actively support and encourage others within your community, recognizing the importance of partnership in your shared faith journey?

_____

_____

_____

_____

2. In what ways have you experienced growth or encouragement through your relationships with other believers, and how can you intentionally invest in these partnerships?

_____

_____

_____

_____

GAME CHANGER

In Colossians 4:2-18, Paul encourages believers to stay devoted to prayer, with hearts rooted in gratitude. This commitment to constant, thankful prayer shapes our perspective, reminding us to rely on God's guidance and strength in every situation. As we remain watchful and alert in prayer, we develop a closer relationship with God, finding peace in His presence and purpose. Gratitude in prayer keeps our focus on God's faithfulness, helping us see His work even in challenging times and preparing us to face the world with a heart grounded in Him.

Paul also calls believers to "walk in wisdom" and "redeem the time," reminding us to make the most of every opportunity to reflect Christ's character to others. Living with intentionality means recognizing that each interaction is an opportunity to demonstrate Christ's love and truth. Making wise choices and using time well builds a stronger witness for Christ and deepens our understanding of His purpose for us.

Finally, Paul's personal greetings and acknowledgment of fellow workers highlight the power of community and partnership in the gospel. He shows us that ministry is not a solo effort but a collaborative journey where believers support, encourage, and uplift one another. Just as Paul valued his companions, we, too, are called to invest in relationships that strengthen our faith and unite us in God's mission.

ONE BIG THING

What is the most significant lesson for you to take with you from this chapter?

_____

_____

_____

_____

_____

_____

_____

_____

_____

_____

_____

_____

IMPACT PRAYER

Lord, Help us to use every moment and interaction as an opportunity to reflect Your love and wisdom to those around us. Teach us to walk intentionally, make the most of our time, and invest in Your church. May our lives reflect Christ, united in purpose and grounded in Your grace. In Jesus' name, Amen.

NOTES:

CONCLUSION

These are the titles of each chapter you studied. Circle the two that carried the most significance to you in your pursuit of being The Complete Coach.

Week 1   Colossians 1:1-8   REJOICES in Maturity

Week 2   Colossians 1:9-14   PRAYS for Maturity

Week 3   Colossians 1:15-20   EXALTS Christ

Week 4   Colossians 1:21-33   REMAINS Steadfast

Week 5   Colossians 1:24-29   LABORS for Others to Mature

Week 6   Colossians 2:1-7   PURSUES Mature Knowledge

Week 7   Colossians 2:8-15   GUARDS Against Deception

Week 8   Colossians 2:16-23   REJECTS Self-made Religion

Week 9   Colossians 3:1-11   PUTS OFF the Old Man

Week 10 Colossians 3:12-16   PUTS ON the New Man

Week 11 Colossians 3:17-4:1   SERVES Christ in Everything

Week 12 Colossians 4:2-18   STRIVES FOR Wisdom

Take this opportunity to write out a prayer to God that articulates your desire to be the complete coach who praises the Lord and leads others to do the same. Especially ask Him to help you grow in the two areas you circled above.

_____

_____

_____

Write down the names and descriptions of the people who participated in this study so that you can remember them and the contribution they made to your spiritual growth.

_____

_____

_____

_____